D0171598

Beneath the Surface

How to Live a Life of Purpose
In Tune with Your Soul

Rabbi Daniel Bortz

Cover Design by Ethan Lew & Isaac Perez

Image of waves in glasses provided by Todd Glaser

This is a delightful book. Daniel Bortz has a contagious sense of wonder and that special gift of being able to take your hand and lead you to those pure and wholesome places in yourself that you forgot existed.

—Rav Avraham Sutton,
author of *Spiritual Technology* and Master Kabbalist

Dedication

This book is dedicated to my incredible parents, David and Helene. You have always supported and encouraged my dreams and are my greatest role models. Thank you for who you are and all that you do for our family. We are so blessed to have you

Introduction

At nineteen, I packed my bags and left my college campus in Southern California for the land of Israel. I couldn't wait to explore the mystery of why I was alive and what my purpose might be on this planet. I felt an inner yearning for a force beyond me, like a flame dancing on a wick, stretching out for a place that transcends it.

Growing up, I had a dream life with everything a child could hope for. But when I became a teenager, none of that helped. I had a deep feeling of emptiness inside. Our inner self, the soul, needs nourishment just as much as our bodies do. It will also cry out when it's starved.

We may desire to transcend the mundane and live elevated lives, but the options presented to us can be temporary distractions at best. Substances may help you escape feelings of existential angst for a short time, but they don't answer a desire deep down to know what your purpose on this earth is.

From the moment I entered the gates of study in Jerusalem, my soul enjoyed a constant stream of profound insights into life that finally quenched my inner thirst and deeply resonated with me. But after years of learning around the world, I realized that the thousands of hours spent poring over Hebrew text hadn't been kind to my eyesight. When I first put on my new pair of glasses, I could see the same world around me as before, but everything was clearer and sharper. The details of nature were vibrant. I noticed beauty in everything that I had been viewing as drab and fuzzy. That day, I appreciated the world like it was new. I realized the time spent learning and growing spiritually had served as glasses for my mind and heart. My focus had turned away from the superficial details around me. I now searched for the deeper truth behind everything I encountered.

In life, the daily grind and our immediate material needs often shout louder than anything spiritual. Our souls are like visiting players in a sports arena where materialism is the home court, every physical desire met with thunderous applause. But deep inside, we desire more. What's our personal calling, our reason for living? This book focuses on how to infuse meaning into every moment, looking at our lives and the world around us beyond the surface layer of reality, and instilling awareness that everything that happens is purposeful and for the best.

***

While our generation craves deep insights into life, we need the ideas to be concise and easily accessible. I've always loved analogies and short stories as vehicles for explanation. While simple, they preserve the deep wisdom behind them. This book attempts to deliver ancient Jewish concepts in an easily attainable way, regardless of your background. To this end, every section was carefully written as concise as possible. Many of these ideas, though, deserve a book of their own to be properly explained. It's easy to read over a story and move on to the next, but I strongly encourage you to spend additional time contemplating an idea here that piques your interest.

In this book, "Torah" refers not only to the *Five Books of Moses*, but also to the oral Torah given through Moses, that's made up of the four layers of explanation: *literal, hinting, Midrashic,* and *mystical* teachings, known as *Pardes*—"The Orchard." The footnotes, in addition to citing sources, provide more in-depth explanation for those interested in exploring deeper.

Many names for *God* are used here interchangeably, such as the *Infinite* and the *Divine*. A name is a way to connect with and describe someone. It doesn't define the individual's essence. So, too names for God describe ways in which He chooses to express Himself. In addition, God is neither masculine nor feminine. I use the pronoun "He" primarily out of custom and convenience.

***

We live in a wondrous universe full of opportunities and lessons to connect to the Infinite. In the book of Job, Job says: "From my flesh I see God." We can learn about God and our lives from every single thing we see. Nature, the human body, galaxies, emotions, and dreams—all can help us to understand and connect with the Divine.

Many insights into the secrets of life can be extracted through traveling and observing the world. But the deepest truths are discovered when staying still and exploring inwardly. We are not bodies that contain souls—we are divine souls housed in bodies. In order to access our souls, we need to look within, developing and elevating our consciousness to higher levels. Through quieting the superficial noise of the outside world and focusing inwardly, we can discover the music of our soul. As James Joyce writes in *Ulysses*: "Shut your eyes and see." Electromagnetic waves may be all around you, but if the radio isn't tuned properly to receive them, nothing will be heard.

There's a story told of a man who had a dream. In that dream, he had a vision of the well-known palace in the capital city of his land. Next to the palace was a bridge, and under that bridge was buried a treasure chest full of gold. When he awoke the next morning, he set out for the capital city. Upon reaching the bridge near the palace, he ran to the exact spot from his dream and started digging. All of a sudden, he heard a shout. A palace guard was standing over him with an angry, but curious look on his face. Without time to think, the poor man explained the dream he had and why he was digging. Laughing, the guard said: "You fool! I too had a dream recently about a buried treasure. It was buried under a small hut on *Stepova Street*, in the village of *Tokmak*. But you don't see me traveling all the way there because of a silly dream!" The guard had described the location of the man's house.

The priceless treasure we seek is already within. It's our *neshamah*—our soul, a divine energy. Your truth lies within; the challenge is to connect and reveal it, and then to live a life in line with that truth.

How do we tune in to our soul and the Divine? And once we feel connected, what are we meant to do with that knowledge in our time here on earth? "Torah" means *instruction*. It was given to us as an instruction manual, explaining how to better our world and become the best version of ourselves. By internalizing the wisdom of the Torah and developing our characters, we can elevate our spiritual awareness day by day, reaching a profoundly deep place within. But the ultimate purpose of this growth is to effect positive change in the world through action.

Although I touch upon it, this book isn't focused on proving the existence of God or the Torah. This book explores ancient Torah teachings that we—regardless of belief or background—can practically learn from, applying its wisdom to enhance our lives today.

For nearly a decade, at the end of every week I would sift through the countless insights from the past days, painfully deciding on only one to share with friends and family. From the sweltering rooftops of Jerusalem to the frozen rooftops of Brooklyn (Internet access wasn't easy to find), I tried to share what I was feeling with others. Even though I knew my rendition of ideas would not do justice to the scope of wisdom behind the original teachings of my teachers, I felt a duty to share inspirational lessons that deeply resonated with me. This book is a selection of these ideas.

I hope that you find within these pages something that uplifts and inspires your journey in life, as it did mine, helping to lift the veil and see beneath the surface layer of reality with a fresh pair of glasses. Through working to see life in a Torah way, may we find the clarity of purpose and strength needed to light up the darkness in our world, revealing the inherent goodness it contains and transforming it into a home for the Divine.

~Please treat this book with respect as many sacred verses
and names are included~

Table of Contents

CHAPTER 1

Art and Music

Fifteen Violins

A music reporter was searching for a good article. After hearing that an exceptional violinist was living in his town, he contacted him for an exclusive interview. The violinist agreed and a date was set. As the interview neared, the reporter received a call from the violinist regretfully informing him that he wouldn't be able to make it.

"There's a special violin ensemble playing a concert on that night. It will be aired on the radio and I can't bear to miss it."

Knowing he could learn a great deal just by observing this great musician, the reporter quickly asked if he could sit and listen to the concert with him.

"Fine," answered the musician. "But I don't want to hear a word during this concert."

The reporter gave his assurance, and at the appointed night, he knocked on the violinist's door.

"Not a word!" reminded the musician, as they settled into their chairs. The radio was turned on and the concert began. The violinist immediately focused intently on the music coming from the radio. The reporter, meanwhile, observed the violinist, searching his facial expressions for any reaction he may have to the melody.

As the music flowed, the reporter found himself enjoying the great beauty of the violins. Each violinist seemed to play off the other, harmonizing seamlessly. He found the music incredibly soothing to his soul. Glancing at the maestro seated by his side, he was surprised to see that he was actually grimacing! He found it hard to believe the violinist was not enjoying the music, but true to his word, he remained silent.

The concert concluded to a standing ovation, and the radio was turned off. The reporter turned to the violinist.

"Sir, I found the concert to have been quite beautiful. But it seemed that you disliked the performance?"

The great violinist turned to the reporter with a look of pity and explained.

"I'm sorry to say, but you enjoyed it because you're an amateur. As an expert of this music, I know that this piece is supposed to be played with fifteen violinists. I could tell there were only fourteen, and the piece was off from beginning to end. This is what ruined it for me."

***

We live in a massive world with over seven billion people, full of noise and action. It's easy to feel our existence matters little. What real difference can my actions make? Would an infinite Being, or the vastness of humanity, really care for the small impact I can make? We wonder where, if at all, we fit in the grand scheme of things.

"Front and center," says God. "Without you, the concert of life is completely ruined."[1] We too must appreciate the individual song every other soul plays.[2]

But remember that your song, your soul's unique purpose, is central to the universe.[3] Your role is so vital that, without its music, the entire symphony of history is incomplete. The grand purpose of the world can

---

[1] "For this reason was man created alone, to teach you that whoever destroys a single soul… Scripture imputes [guilt] to him as though he had destroyed a complete world; and whoever preserves a single soul… Scripture ascribes [merit] to him as though he had preserved a complete world" (Talmud, Sanhedrin 37a).

[2] [Ben Azzai] would also say: "Do not scorn any man, and do not discount any thing. For there is no man who has not his hour, and no thing that has not its place" (Ethics of Our Fathers, 4:3).

[3] Every single person is obligated to say: "The world was created for my sake" (Ibid).

only be realized through your contribution. The puzzle is completed with your piece.[4]

The Mona Lisa

Why are high-quality paintings so much more monetarily valuable than high-quality photographs?

In terms of accuracy, a photograph is certainly better! If you want to capture exactly what the Pacific Ocean looks like during a sunset, snap a photograph. A painting is merely an interpretation, a portrayal of a scene. It's never perfectly accurate. So why are paintings able to sell for millions of dollars while photos sell for substantially less?

We appreciate a painting *because* it isn't perfect. A limited human exerts intense effort and skill for long periods of time in an attempt to capture reality. Each painting is unique to its artist, expressing a distinct personality, vision, and talent.

Now we can understand a more meaningful question: Why would an infinite God value a finite human's actions and intentions, especially when compared with the perfect service of flawless heavenly angels, purely spiritual beings? Human beings live imperfect lives. We rarely express our true potential, often preferring superficial actions to lives of truth. To live a perfect life is impossible, and the angels succeed where we fail. So why did God give the Torah to humans, desiring a relationship with us?

The powerful reason is that God desires *paintings*, not photographs. Your life is being painted; it isn't a perfect portrayal of goodness and truth, but it's your own unique expression of your soul. It's your contribution to the world and to God. An artist expends much sweat and toil to achieve his goal, and every brushstroke is essential to the final product. It may not be perfect, but that's precisely what separates us from angels.

---

[4] Throughout the Psalms of King David, God is referred to as the *Choirmaster*, orchestrating the symphony that is life, made up of every life and detail of the universe performing its role (Psalm 20, 51, et al).

Angels are God's *photographers*. They are perfect servants, but they are also stagnant, without progression or improvement to a higher level. We, however, have the ability to refine and uplift ourselves, striving to reach lofty goals.[5] Our lives are spent beautifying our individual paintings by beautifying the world, adding in kindness and refining our characters, all the while doing our best to avoid damaging our masterpiece. For when our paintings are finally complete, do we want them displayed at a 99¢ store or at the Louvre?

***

There once lived a villager who needed a special favor that could only be granted by the king himself. Unfortunately, the only way to gain admittance to see the king was by bringing a special gift, and this villager was poor. One day, he thought of a great idea for a gift, and off he went to the palace. Upon entering its inner chamber, the villager stood before the king and his subjects, all eyes fixed upon him and the covered gift in his hands.

Slowly, the villager pulled the black cloak off the gift, revealing a parrot inside a cage. The crowd present gasped in unison upon seeing such an underwhelming gift. In reply, the villager reached into his pocket, took out a cracker, and fed it to the parrot.

"Long live the king!" chirped the parrot.

Everyone turned to the king and found him bent over and laughing hysterically.

"This is the greatest gift I have ever received! Please do it again!"

The king immediately granted the man his wish.

***

What was so great about this gift? The king could have hired thousands of servants to sing his praises and wish him long life. Why was he so

---

[5] Human potential is infinitely greater than that of angels because of our source in the Divine. While angels, together with the rest of Creation, were *spoken* into existence, regarding human beings the Torah states, "And (God) breathed into his nostrils the soul of life" (Genesis 2:7). Speech comes from a more external aspect of our beings, which is why we can speak all day long without tiring. But blowing out air stems from deep within. God has no "mouth" or "breath." The Torah uses this analogy to symbolize just how deep within God our divine souls emanate. See: Tanya, Iggeret Hakodesh, epistle 23.

impressed with the praises of an animal? He enjoyed it so much because it was a *novelty*. It was a total shock to see a bird imitating a human.

God didn't create a world so that holy people could do holy things. He created a world where *unholy* people could do holy things. It's because we are flawed that our good deeds are so precious to God, bringing greater joy than could any angelic being.

The Piano Player

Imagine walking into a fancy department store. As you enter, you hear a beautiful piano melody. Searching through clothes, you mentally file away the music as coming from one of those pianos whose keys are automated to play on their own. All of a sudden, you hear one of the notes momentarily deviate from the flow of the song. Even after the rhythm returns to its usual melody, you realize that there was someone sitting at the piano playing the keys all along.

***

There are two important principles in Judaism that require constant effort to internalize. The first is divine providence—the perspective that God isn't hanging out in heaven watching the world indifferently from afar, bag of popcorn in hand. He's directing everything, intimately involved in every detail of our lives, from traffic delays and health problems to job promotions and meeting our soul mates.

The Jewish mystics take it a step further: God even decides the direction in which each and every leaf falls from a tree! Like a loving and vigilant parent who cares for his young child, He leaves no circumstance or detail to chance.

But how often do we notice the conductor behind the orchestra that is life? In our story of the music in the department store, the glitches in the piano music symbolize the moments of revealed Providence in our lives that are out of the ordinary, going against the natural course of things. These unique moments are not meant to remain isolated highlights of our week. They shine a light on the fact that God is behind everything always. We need only be sensitive enough to notice these special events, realizing them as opportunities to glimpse behind the veil of nature and chance.[6] As King Solomon, the wisest of men, taught: "In his heart a man plans his course, but the Lord directs his steps."[7]

If God directs everything, then where is our free choice?

The Talmud states: "All is in the hands of heaven, except for the awe of heaven."[8] Free choice lies in our effort, moral decision making toward our fellow human beings, and in our relationship with God. Our external circumstances are out of our control. We do, however, have control over how we respond to them. A train delay or turbulence midflight shouldn't create stress, for it, too has a specific purpose for our ultimate benefit.

This leads us to Judaism's second important principle—joy. Living joyfully is vital to life. The two principles of belief in divine providence and living joyfully are intimately connected. Many of us are dissatisfied because we feel our lives are arbitrary and lack genuine purpose and direction.

What if we were aware that every encounter in our day-to-day lives have a specific purpose? That traffic jam is specifically designed to improve on your capacity for patience, which can later be used in your relationships where it matters. That depressed cashier and waiter serving you is an opportunity for you to brighten their day with a smile and kind word. Each moment of our lives is unique with specific opportunities to affect change. Nobody else in the world will interact with the same people, in the same way, that you can.

Every day is another opportunity to refine ourselves and the world. In Jewish tradition, the moment we awake, we express thanks with a short prayer, gratefully acknowledging the unique opportunity another day affords us to fulfill our life's mission.

---

[6] The numerical equivalent of the Hebrew word "nature"— *teva*— is 86. Significantly, the Hebrew word for "God"—*E-lohim*— is also 86. "Nature" is just the repetition of constant miracles.

[7] Proverbs 16:9.

[8] Talmud, Berachot 33b.

CHAPTER 2

Awareness

The Nature of Nature

To gain insight into the inner emotions and intentions of an artist, we need to intensely study their artwork. To understand the One who designed the universe, we also need to look deeply into that Artist's work, the nature of existence.

Children constantly wonder, often out loud, at the world around them: *Why's the sky blue? Where does rain come from? Why do I have five toes?* As we grow older, we tend to lose our sense of wonder when looking at our surroundings. We've simply become accustomed to what we see and experience as just being there. Everything is *natural*, meaning something consistent that keeps to a certain unchanging pattern. Flowers grow in the spring; leaves change color in autumn; and snow falls in the winter. But who instituted this orderly set of *laws of nature*? Why isn't existence complete chaos? Would we expect a massive explosion in a room to produce exquisitely beautiful order? And yet, this is what the Big Bang explosion did, producing an incredibly tuned universe of life. Nature is just a cycle of miracles, unimpressive because of its consistency.

When we see a painting we wonder what the artist intended. What story is being told and what is the artist trying to express? Let us do the same when looking at the universe, the most beautiful and complex work of art imaginable.

What is the true nature of nature? The Hebrew word for "nature" is *teva*, which has the dual meaning in Hebrew of "sunken" or "drowned." Since Hebrew words connote function and the inner truth of something,[9] this definition of *teva* indicates that God's existence is *concealed* within nature, like an object that has sunken into water, submerged and hidden from the naked eye.

How can we develop a more conscious awareness of an artist behind the painting? As children, we wonder at everything around us. But as we age and learn more about the world, our minds classify everything we see in categories: *That's a bird, that's a tree, and those are roses. They're nice, but there's nothing new here, I've seen them all before.* What if the next time we see something in nature—a flower, a tree, a bird, or a human face—we refuse to immediately label it and move on with our day, unimpressed? Instead, why not look at an apple and think: *What is this round red thing with refreshing taste that gives me a boost in energy?* See a hummingbird and wonder at its magnificent makeup and movement. *This didn't have to exist here at all.* Just because we've observed something before doesn't make it any less wondrous.[10] We can gaze at a reality beneath the surface by looking with a fresh, new perspective.

As strange as it sounds, by not labeling and immediately filing things away in our mental cabinets as standard, we can come to appreciate the unique beauty and brilliant design of everything we see. This also applies to our human interactions, even with people we've known for a long while. Just because we've filed a person into our mental filing cabinets as being

---

[9]   In Hebrew, the word for "thing/object" is *davar*, while "word" is also *davar*. Jewish mysticism explains that the Hebrew words God used when speaking the universe into form are invested into and continually enlivening each object. This is why each Hebrew name describes the essence of that thing. See Tanya, The Gate of Unity and Faith, ch. 1.

[10] See Tolle, Eckhart. *A New Earth.* New York: Penguin Books, 2005. p. 5.

a certain type doesn't represent the full depth of the person. We're always able to delve further into the significance of every being.[11]

Many may imagine God as a Being detached from the universe. This perception can make the workings of our world also appear separate from Him, when in fact they may be *expressions* of Him. Do we unintentionally treat God the same way we do with everything else, typecasting and filing away an incorrect image in our minds of who He is? Language is very limiting. Even the name "God" conjures up for many an Invisible Being floating in space, or an old judgmental king in the sky. Let's step back from the painting and reevaluate with a fresh pair of eyes.

There's more depth in most things than we see at first glance. Use a few moments in your busy day to marvel at the art that is our world. This can enrich your life with wonder and meaning, helping to gain insight into the profound artist behind the universe.

The Professor

A university student enrolled in a philosophy course. He enjoyed learning from his professor, who frequently included spiritual themes during his lectures. One day, the student took his seat, and as the class settled down and quieted their chatting and laughing, the professor stood at his podium without saying a word. Minutes ticked by, and the professor had still said nothing. Everyone looked at one another, confused, thinking their professor was deranged. Finally, after considerable squirming and uncomfortable silence, the professor began.

"Do you hear that?"

Now they were certain. This poor guy must have lost his mind.

---

[11] "Who is wise? One who learns from everybody." Ethics of our Fathers, 4:1. "Do not scorn any man, and do not discount any thing. For there is no man who has not his hour, and no thing that has not its place." Ethics of our Fathers, 4:3.

This student wondered what his teacher could possibly be referring to. He began to notice that, in fact, he had never heard the humming of the ceiling fan before, and after the professor asked a third time, he spoke up.

"Are you referring to the humming of the fan?"

The professor smiled. "Yes. It was always there, but since all of you were so busy chatting, you never noticed it. Class is dismissed, have a great day."

Everyone quickly filed out, ecstatic at the early dismissal. But the student who had spoken up remained in his seat.

What message was the professor trying to get across? He approached his teacher and asked him to explain his thinking.

"We're so busy talking, moving, and being distracted by everything around us," explained the professor. *"We never take a moment to stop and hear the hum of our inner beings, our soul. The universe too has a soul, a spiritual energy that pervades it. But like the constant hum of the fan, we're too distracted to notice. The purpose of our days would surely be different if we did."*[12]

The Eye of Infinity

Early in the Torah, we are introduced to the first Jew, Abraham, arguably the greatest revolutionary in the history of civilization. Introducing monotheism to the world, Abraham burns with a desire to teach the pagan world his belief in a single divine power that controls all else. Until Abraham, man chose the sun, moon, stars, and images of wood and stone as their gods. The *Midrash* describes one of the ways Abraham came to monotheism at a young age.

---

[12] This is reminiscent of the 2007 study conducted by Gene Weingarten of the *Washington Post*, where he had world-renowned violinist, Joshua Bell, play six Bach pieces on his $3.5 million violin right next to the metro station in Washington, DC. Hardly a person stopped to listen or donate, merely two days after tickets to his concert had gone for 100 dollars. One conclusion we can take from this Pulitzer Prize-winning study, is if humans are able to overlook one of the best musicians of our time playing his best music, how many other precious aspects of life might we be missing?

***

Seeing the sun's powerful rays beaming onto the earth, blinding his eyes, Abraham first believed the sun to be God. But as night came, the sun left and the moon took over. The moon must be God, he thought. As this cycle continued, Abraham observed a shift in the orbit of the planets and a rhythm of movement in the nature around him. Seeing each force moving in sync, with none in full control of the others, Abraham concluded that there must be one directing all of them, whose presence—while hidden in nature—was recognizable through His design.

***

With a much greater understanding today of the intricacies that make up life, it's easier to recognize an intelligent Designer than it was for Abraham. Let's look at one simple example: the human eye.

"What is happening inside your eye as you are reading these words? Light passes through the front of the eye (the pupil) and through the lens. This light goes toward the back of the eye (the retina), where in a space less than one square inch, there are approximately one hundred million small machines shaped like rods. Every rod is connected by a nerve fiber to the brain. The rods contain a chemical substance called "visual purple" (rhodopsin). When the light reaches the rod, it causes the visual purple to break down. This breakdown generates several millionths of a volt of electricity. This electricity is transmitted to the brain through the optic nerve at about 300 mph. The brain interprets the signals coming in, identifies what is being seen, and remembers the image. The entire process is completed in about two thousandths of a second!"[13]

---

[13] Lipman, Dov Moshe. *Discover.* New York: Feldheim, 2006. p. 5. Charles Darwin writes in *The Origin of Species* – ch. VI: "To suppose that the eye with all its inimitable contrivances for adjusting the focus to different distances, for admitting different amounts of light, and for the correction of spherical and chromatic aberration, could have been formed by natural selection, seems, I freely confess, absurd in the highest degree." He later explains the natural evolution of the eye. However, he concludes: "How a nerve comes to be sensitive to light, hardly concerns us more than how life itself originated."

There's so much we can learn from the intricacies of our bodies and the world around us. The ability to appreciate detail is a crucial aspect of spiritual experience and mindfulness, cultivating a feeling of gratitude. Imagine if, when you ate, you were conscious of everything that went into your meal. As you bite into a bagel with cream cheese and lox, imagine what it took for that food to reach you. The wheat for the bagel had to be grown and nurtured properly for months with the right soil, water, and sunlight, later processed into flour and baked. The cream cheese originated from the milk of a cow that was born and nurtured for years before its milking. The lox came from fish traversing the ocean, perhaps thousands of miles away from you. This mindfulness generates a sensitive approach to eating, appreciating where our food comes from and the life energy we receive through consuming it.

The Torah teaches: "Man is a miniature world,"[14] meaning that everything in nature can be found on some level within a human being. When standing in nature, which three predominant colors are generally seen? Brown (earth), green (grass and trees), and blue (sky). These mimic the three predominant eye colors of brown, green and blue. On a deeper level, just as the body is a vessel and conduit for the expression of the soul, so, too is the earth energized by a Godly energy that expresses itself through every aspect.

Let's examine the central location of the human senses—the head and face. Each sense found there *ascends* in ability and power. A shout leaving your mouth can be heard one to two miles away at most. But

[14] Midrash Tanchuma, Pekudei Siman 3. This idea is seen in many places. Just as the world is made up of a majority of water, so too is the human body. "The rabbis taught: The creation of the world was like the creation of humanity, for everything that God created in the world, God created in the human being. The heavens are the head of humankind, the sun and the moon are the human eyes, the stars are the hair on the human head" (Otzar haMidrashim, Olam Katan 406). "One who knows the secret of the human soul, and the structure of the human body, is able to understand something of the upper worlds, for the human being is in the image of a small world" (Sefer ha-Temunah fol. 25a). "Just as God fills the whole world, so the soul fills the body" (Talmud, Berachot 10a). "Whomever saves a single life, saves an entire world" (Mishnah, Sanhedrin 4:5). See Tikkunei Zohar 100b, et al.

your nose can smell smoke from a fire from hundreds of miles away. The ears can hear farther: In 1883, an eruption in Krakatoa was reportedly heard three thousand miles away. The eyes can gaze at the moon, stars, and sun (be careful) millions of miles away. And then there's the brain, able to contemplate ideas that transcend the dimensions of the universe entirely.

Abraham's investigations into the fine-tuning of nature led him to an awareness of a Creator. This initial wonder and excitement led him on a lifelong pursuit of truth and righteousness. All of us at one time have felt a sense of awe while in nature. Gazing from a mountain peak while looking out over the waves of a vast ocean, we may have felt a greater force than ourselves at work in the universe. Like our forefather Abraham, we, too shouldn't let these moments of inspiration dissipate. We should translate these moments of inspiration into tangible action, living life with an awareness of a greater purpose in our everyday lives.

Technology

Our generation is witnessing constant advances and innovations in technology. Is all of this change for the good?

We are witnessing greater advancements in technology at a more rapid rate than any past generation. As is true with most things, technology when misused can lead to the worsening of our society and quality of life. While social media connects people, it can also be used to bully and harass others.

But technology also presents an amazing opportunity to encourage and uplift others. Digital communication even has the power to help topple oppressive regimes as seen in the *Arab Spring*. There's no shortage of degrading and useless material on the Internet, but the Internet also makes insightful and thought provoking information accessible to us as never before. One viral video can inspire worldwide positive change.

Could it be that these advancements have come about specifically in our generation in order to be used for a greater purpose and awareness?[15] When looked at on a deeper level, technology can even be studied to come to a greater awareness of the Divine.

Through modern advancement, we can gain new insight into the ancient mystical tenet that every aspect of reality in the universe is being vitalized constantly by a flow of divine energy. Kabbalah teaches that the spiritual DNA of all matter is a Godly Energy that courses through it, and without this, physical matter would simply cease to exist.[16] Anyone learning this concept even a hundred years ago would be justified in viewing it with skepticism. *How can this wooden table be made up of spiritual energy? It's a physical object that I can see and touch!*

Today we know better. A table is more than the piece of wood we see with our naked eye. High-powered quantum microscopes allow us to observe the trillions of atoms that make up a table—protons, neutrons, and electrons—and zooming in further, the subatomic particles that comprise those atoms. And we haven't yet reached the ultimate core of reality; we are still exploring deeper.

Science and technology enable our eyes to see further. From the complexity of the outermost galaxies down to the innermost intricacies of

---

[15] In the Torah portion of Noah, Genesis 7:11 states: "In the six-hundredth year in the life of Noah… all wellsprings of the great deep burst open, and the windows of heaven were opened…" The Zohar Part I, 117a, interprets this verse in a prophetic fashion, alluding to matters beyond the flood of the time: "In the 600th year of the 6th millennium [1840 CE] the upper gates of wisdom will be opened and also the wellsprings of wisdom below. This will prepare the world for the 7th millennium like a person prepares himself on Friday for Shabbat, as the sun begins to wane. So it will be here." By "upper" wisdom, the Zohar may have been alluding to the spiritual revolution of the Chassidic movement and teachings of the Baal Shem Tov that spread widely in the nineteenth century, while the "lower" wisdom probably refers to the Industrial Revolution of the nineteenth century.

[16] An interesting Hollywood portrayal of such a concept is seen at the end of the first *The Matrix* movie. While not completely accurate, many Torah concepts are explored here. Regarding the illusion that what we see is all there is, *Morpheus* tells *Neo*: "It is the world that has been pulled over your eyes to blind you from the truth." Neo later sees how all of reality is made up of a code.

14

the workings of the human body, today it is easier to see a divine order and unity in the universe than ever before.

"What is the way to have love and awe of God? Whenever one contemplates the great wonders of God's works and creations..."[17] We can thank modern science and technology for a deeper awareness of these wonders. As physicists dig deeper into the makeup of matter, they may end up turning to the writings of the Jewish mystics to find out their essence.

"To my mind, there must be at the bottom of it all, not an utterly simple equation, but an utterly simple idea. And to me that idea, when we finally discover it, will be so compelling, and so inevitable, so beautiful, we will all say to each other, 'How could it have ever been otherwise?'"[18]

---

[17] Maimonides, Foundations of the Torah 2:2.

[18] John Wheeler was a professor at Princeton University and a visionary physicist who helped invent the theory of nuclear fission and gave black holes their name. For more on this "simple idea", see: Schroeder, Gerald. *The Hidden Face of God.* New York: Free Press, 2002.

CHAPTER 3

Self

Happiness

"When the month of Adar enters, one must increase in joy."[19]

To *increase* in joy implies that we're already expected to be joyful and only need to add to it in this month. King David, who lived an incredibly difficult life, taught: "Serve God in joy."[20] But is this a fair expectation?

It sounds nice in theory. As children we were upbeat, laughing often without a care in the world. But as we grow, we start to feel like the weight of the world is on our shoulders, worrying about our health, bills, relationships, and a myriad of other daily pressures. What may be needed is a change in perspective.

From our narrow vantage point, we may feel that life owes us. If something is lacking, I feel it isn't fair. Why does that person have it all and I don't? But what if we took the opposite approach in thinking and asked ourselves: Do we really *deserve* anything at all? Everything good we have is actually an unearned gift, including life itself!

---

[19] Taanit 29a.

[20] Psalms 100:2. The *Code of Jewish Law* begins with the tenet: "I place God before me always." If one is supposed to serve God at all times, and one is to be joyful when serving, then 1+1 = 2, and we are to be joyful at all times.

When describing the greatest prophet who ever lived, the Torah states: "There was no other prophet who arose in Israel like Moses, whom the Lord knew face to face."[21] Surprisingly, it also states: "Now this man Moses was extremely humble, more so than any person on earth."[22]

Isn't it odd that the most admired person—who was also the greatest leader of his time, more iconic in his day than Michael Jordan and Albert Einstein combined—was also the most humble?

The Sages explain that Moses was able to live this way because he understood that all of his great qualities were simply gifts from God.[23]

The primary qualities that bring success to a fashion model, a brilliant mathematician, or an incredible athlete have little to do with effort. They are gifts from above.[24] In his humility, Moses thought that if God had given his special attributes to others, perhaps they would have used them better. Feeling humble doesn't equate to having a lower self-esteem. It means having total awareness of each of your talents, while understanding that they are gifts that come with a responsibility to use them out for a greater purpose.

If everything we have is a gift, feeling we're unfairly lacking something can lose its sting. If this thing was necessary for my mission and purpose in this lifetime, then I would have it.[25]

In truth, we are all wealthy beyond our wildest dreams. If you were offered five million dollars for your pair of eyes, would you take it? The

---

[21] Deuteronomy 34:10.

[22] Numbers 12:3.

[23] Another answer is that it's actually *because* Moses was the greatest prophet who spoke with God "face to face" (meaning on an intimate level) that he was the most humble. The reason our egos inflate is because we're unaware of a greater power. But imagine we always had a deep awareness of an infinite divine force? How intensely humbling that would be.

[24] It's true that much effort is exerted to succeed in any field, regardless of how talented someone is. But the natural brilliance, athleticism, and beauty that are being worked with haven't been earned.

[25] It's true as well that the Mitzvah of prayer is primarily to ask God for our needs. Together with this is the belief that if our request isn't fulfilled, it's because we didn't truly need it for our life mission.

true value of what we naturally possess is priceless. If we lived our lives with this awareness, that everything we have—down to our very breaths—are wonderful gifts, our quality of life would brighten.[26]

This is why Judaism places a great focus on daily prayer. A consistent word in the prayer book is *hoda'ah,* meaning "gratitude" or "acknowledgment." Blessings before and after eating, prayers after restroom use and after safe travel, all reinforce an awareness of how lucky we are for every little blessing in our lives.

Ferraris and six-pack abs may be nice, but what we naturally own is far more precious; the things that can't be bought. Material acquisitions are temporary, while kind actions and spiritual pursuits are everlasting, for their effects live on in the permanent realm of the spiritual.[27] Our ability today to live and impact this world is the most precious gift of all, something worthy of smiling about.[28]

Perspective

In eighteenth-century Eastern Europe, there lived two brothers who were Hasidic Masters with great followings, Reb Elimelech and Reb Zusha. They traveled anonymously to scattered towns and villages to inspire their inhabitants. Reb Zusha was known to say that upon his death and entrance into the heavenly court, he wouldn't be asked: "Why weren't you like Abraham, Isaac, and Jacob?"

Instead he would be asked: "Why weren't you like Zusha? Why didn't you live up to your individual potential?"

As often happened to Jewish citizens of Europe in those days, on one of their journeys the brothers were unfairly arrested and thrown into prison. With faith that God orchestrates everything in life, the brothers accepted their fate in good spirit. But during the first day of imprisonment, Elimelech noticed that his brother appeared downcast.

---

[26] To internalize this concept deeper, see: *It's All a Gift,* by Miriam Adahan and *Thank You – Gratitude: Formulas, Stories, and Insights,* by Rabbi Zelig Pliskin.

[27] Tanya ch. 25.

[28] See the online video entitled *Gratitude* by Louie Schwartzberg that illustrates this beautifully.

"What's the matter Zusha? You know this is all for the best!"

"It's not that," Zusha answered with a sigh. Pointing to the communal toilet bucket in the shared prison cell, he explained:

"We can't pray here. Jewish law states that one is forbidden to recite holy words of prayer next to such foul areas. How can I enjoy any moment of my day when I can't be serving God properly?"

"But my brother," Reb Elimelech replied gently. "The same God that so desires your prayers also desires that in this situation you not pray. By not praying, you are serving Him!"

Reb Zusha's frown turned into a wide grin.

"You're absolutely right!"

Grabbing his brother by the arm, Reb Zusha began dancing around the room, singing with great joy. Attracted by the festive dancing and singing, the other prisoners ran to join in.

The vicious prison guards rushed to the scene and asked the first prisoner they saw for the reason behind the celebration. With a laugh, he pointed to the waste bucket.

"If that's the case, we'll get rid of their joy immediately!"

The guards grabbed the bucket and tossed it out of the room.

***

There are two classic sayings of the Sages: "Joy breaks through all barriers" and "Think good and it will be good."[29]

Far from a naïve notion, many have noted the positive impact our thinking can have on reality. Quantum physicists have observed that our minds and consciousness can actually affect the physical circumstances around us.[30] In modern medicine, many argue the power the mind has

---

[29] In the original Yiddish: *Tracht gut, vet zein gut* — 'Think good and it will be good," was a known teaching of the 3rd Lubavitcher Rebbe, the *Tzemach Tzedek* [1789-1866].

[30] This is illustrated in the double-slit experiment segment of the 2004 film, *What the Bleep Do We Know!? Down the Rabbit Hole.*

on the health of the body, citing the placebo effect and other studies. By approaching life with optimism and joy, regardless of the situations thrown our way, we are able to affect an openly favorable outcome.[31] This age-old Jewish concept of the power of positivity to affect one's reality is today known by some as the Law of Attraction, and was recently adapted into a self-help book that sold nineteen million copies.[32]

If we approach life's challenges with optimism like Reb Zusha and Reb Elimelech, we may yet see the open and revealed good that comes from staring down darkness with a big smile.

The Struggler

Are there things about yourself you wish you could change? Do you wish you were more patient, caring, selfless, courageous, kind? We all have something we struggle with. Trying to improve our characteristics can feel like an exercise in futility. At times, we feel more refined and genuinely inspired, only to immediately fall down into negative desires and actions. Why in life must we deal with such strong negative impulses? There's an ancient Chinese tale that can shed some light on this.

***

There once lived an elderly woman who, every morning, would carry two buckets to the river to retrieve water. One bucket was whole, while the other was full of cracks and holes. The cracked bucket began to feel terrible, and it cried to its owner:

"I'm such a failure. I'm such a loser. Every day when you return, I barely have a third of the water of a regular bucket!"

The elderly lady replied: "Tomorrow on our walk, I want you to pay closer attention to your surroundings."

---

[31] Even though all that happens is for the best, the good may be hidden. One's optimistic outlook can influence that the outcome becomes good in a *revealed* way, like the waste bucket being tossed out.

[32] Byrne, Ronda. *The Secret*. Oregon: Beyond Words Publishing, 2006.

The next day, she ventured off to the river as usual with her two buckets, but this time, the flawed bucket took time to look around and noticed a vast array of beautiful flowers.

"Wow! These flowers are incredible!"

The woman turned to the cracked bucket and said with a smile, "It's because of your holes that these flowers have been watered and blossomed."

***

In 1797, an integral book of Jewish mysticism, titled *Tanya*, was published in Russia. It revolutionized the way we can view our daily struggles with negative impulses. Before learning Tanya, it's easy to think that we have a split personality; how is it possible to mess up only minutes after feeling so inspired and spiritually uplifted? A minute ago, we were feeling so positive and selfless, and now we're driven by selfish passions. What's the point of trying to improve ourselves if we will never attain perfection?

The *Tanya*'s answer is simple.

Who said God wants you to be perfect? God desires the struggle! Be a warrior. Humanity's hero is the *struggler*, not the saint. Don't view your imperfections, blemishes, negative impulses, and desires as curses. By struggling and working to overcome your challenges—albeit not every time—you bring incredible light into the world. These are our beautiful flowers derived from the occasional victory over the inner or outer darkness.

Just as a candle's light appears more powerful when lit in darkness, our good deeds in this world of spiritual concealment have a more powerful effect. If we only focus on what's wrong with ourselves, it's easy to become despondent. We are meant to have a negative side and to struggle with and use it for good.[33] The important thing is to never become complacent. We must always battle our selfish and destructive sides through selfless kindness and a positive attitude.[34] Just entering the battle of life by working to be better is a heroic endeavor.

"Who is strong? One who conquers his evil inclination. As it is written, 'One who is slow to anger is better than the mighty, and one who rules over their spirit than one who conquers a city.'"[35]

Seeing the Positive

The famous Nazi hunter, Simon Wiesenthal, once spoke at a conference of European Rabbis in Bratislava, Slovakia. The Rabbis presented the ninety-one-year-old Wiesenthal with an award. Visibly moved, he told the audience a story.

***

I was in Mauthausen shortly after liberation. Rabbi Eliezer Silver, head of the Union of Orthodox Rabbis of North America, visited our camp as part of a mission to offer aid and comfort to the survivors. The Rabbi organized a special service and invited me to join other survivors in prayer. I declined his offer, and explained.

In the concentration camp, there was someone who had managed to smuggle in a prayer book. At first, I greatly admired him for his courage. But soon, I realized to my dismay that he was renting out this book to people in exchange for food. Many gave him their last piece of bread for a few minutes with the book. This man, who was very thin and emaciated when the book renting began, was soon eating so much that he died before anyone else because his system couldn't handle it. If this is how religious Jews behave, I don't want to have anything to do with a prayer book.

---

[33] For example, we are told that Jacob's warrior brother, Esau, and the holy King David were of similar complexion and personality. However, while Esau used his fiery nature for evil purposes, King David used his equally passionate nature for good, fighting to protect his people and transforming his urges toward the Divine. See Bereishit Rabbah, ch. 63.

[34] The Sages define the core difference between impurity and holiness as selfishness vs. selflessness.

[35] Ethics of Our Fathers 4:1. Proverbs 16:32.

As I turned to walk away, Rabbi Silver touched me on the shoulder. Speaking gently in Yiddish, he said:

"Why do you look at the one who used his prayer book to take food out of the mouths of the starving? Look at all the people who were willing to give up their last piece of bread just to pray one time. That's the true power of the soul and of prayer."

Rabbi Silver then embraced me. The next day I went to the service.

***

This event from the Holocaust can teach us many things, including the beauty of having faith even in the darkest of circumstances. But it especially illustrates the importance of seeing the good in others. When our shirts have a stain, we focus solely on it, ignoring the rest of the shirt. It's much easier to see the flaws in a person than to notice all of their good traits.

News today is seldom positive, and the world is depicted as full of evil. Mr. Rogers, the famous children's television host, once remarked:

"When I was a boy and I would see scary things in the news, my mother would tell me to look for the helpers. You will always find people who are helping. To this day, especially in times of disaster, I remember her words and am always comforted by knowing that there are still so many helpers—so many caring people in this world."

As much evil as we observe in the world today, equally visible are the countless individuals working tirelessly to help those around them in new and innovative ways. There's a "goodness revolution" today. Innumerable nonprofits and social entrepreneurs are dedicating their lives to curing problems worldwide on a greater scale than ever before. Instead of dwelling on the negativity in the world, let's redouble our efforts to become the source of positive change we wish to see.

Eternal Value

A simple villager was walking the cobblestone streets of his town when he happened upon a crumpled treasure map. An X marked a location that was described as full of diamonds!

The man rushed home and explained everything to his excited family and hurriedly made plans to travel to the distant island. He borrowed a huge sum of money to charter a ship for the journey to this remote area of the world. Taking leave from his family, he promised to return with great wealth for them all.

After weeks at sea following the map, the ship finally approached the shore. He couldn't believe his eyes—the beach was glimmering with countless diamonds! Arriving on the sand, he began filling every pocket he had. After an hour, the man realized he was famished. He walked into the first tavern and ordered everything his heart desired. Satisfied, he generously offered a diamond as payment for the meal.

The owner looked him up and down in dismay.

"Is this some kind of joke? All of us have diamonds. This is worthless!"

Shocked, the man asked, if not diamonds, what then was valuable on this island?

"Chicken fat, of course," came the reply.

Vowing to pay his bill at a later date, the man staggered out of the tavern in a state of disbelief, with pockets full of now-worthless diamonds.

He wandered the streets, noticing countless stores selling chicken fat with different functions. He quickly realized that the people had no shoes or sandals made of chicken fat. He took a loan and fashioned several pairs, which sold quickly. In time, he turned his shoemaking into a thriving business. Soon he was the wealthiest man on the island, with endless amounts of chicken fat. Rich and famous, he had the success he had always dreamed of. Now it was time to return home and share his accumulated wealth with his family. He paid for a fleet of ships and loaded them up with his entire wealth of chicken fat. He sent word ahead to his family that he was returning with untold riches.

As the ships neared his village, from a distance he could see his family waiting at the dock. But to his surprise, instead of looking excited at the amazing wealth he had accrued, they were holding their noses and grimacing! The smell of rotting chicken fat was being swept ashore. Only then did he realize his failure to bring home any diamonds. He only had loads of now-worthless chicken fat.

With a heavy heart, the man sat down on his ship and wept. With shaking hands and a glimmer of hope, he reached into his pocket and found a few remaining diamonds.

***

We were placed in this world for a set number of years to accomplish as much good as possible. Like diamonds covering a beach, good deeds and mitzvot[36] are precious. But focusing on a life of good and values isn't properly valued in today's culture, where greater importance is placed on social and material success. We're prone to becoming distracted by what society values, chasing after a transient fortune. Let's not spend our lives focusing on chicken fat but on the truly valuable attainments that can never be taken away.

***

There was a king who had a favorite advisor. The other advisors were very jealous of him, so they plotted to slander him to the king. They had overheard him speaking of his personal fortune, which they knew was far less than his real worth. They informed the king that this man had a deceptive character. Upon hearing this, the king called his trusted advisor in, giving him a chance to set the record straight.

"I own $2,000 dinars," the advisor calmly answered the king.

"I'm surprised," said the king. "Aren't you worth over 10,000 dinars?"

"My majesty, I'm worth 2,000," he reiterated.

Shocked and angered by this lie, the king ordered his possessions seized and his advisor sent to prison. As he was being led out, the advisor asked to have one more word with the king.

---

[36] Mitzvot are commandments in the Torah. The Hebrew word mitzvah is related to the word *tzavta*—connection. Mitzvot are deeds on earth that connect us to the Infinite.

"Your majesty, I didn't lie. The 2,000 dinars I said were mine refers to the exact amount I've given to charity during this past year. That currency I own forever. The rest of my wealth isn't mine, and the proof is that you were able to take it from me whenever you wanted to. So was it ever truly mine?"

The king smiled and released his advisor.

***

The possessions we attain in this lifetime come and go.[37] The pharaohs of Ancient Egypt liked to be buried together with all of their wealth to accompany them into the next world. Judaism rejects the idea that any of our material wealth carries over. It's our good thoughts, words, and deeds that last forever.[38] This is all we can ever truly own. How we've grown, what we've given, and how we've impacted the lives of other people is the ultimate measure of our worth.

True Pleasure—True Worth

Rabbi Jacob would say:

"A single moment of repentance and good deeds in this world is greater than all of the World to Come. And a single moment of bliss in the World to Come is greater than all of the present world."[39]

This poses a puzzling contradiction. The first teaching seems to ascribe greater value to this world than to the world to come, while the second teaching does the opposite. Should our focus be on this life or the next?

---

[37] *A traveler was passing through a town in Eastern Europe where a renowned sage lived, and decided to make a special effort to meet him. Upon reaching the Rabbi's home, the traveler was shocked to see how humbly such a famous personality lived. The peeling walls of the living room included only one rickety table, two wooden chairs and an old bookcase full of books. He looked at the sage in wonderment and asked, "Rabbi! Where is all of your furniture?"*
"My dear friend," the Rabbi replied. "Where is all of your furniture?"
Caught off guard by such a strange question, the traveler responded,
"But I'm only passing through here!"
The sage replied, "I too am only passing through."

[38] Tanya, ch. 25. "This union is eternal in the upper spheres, for He and His Will are above time."

[39] Ethics of Our Fathers, 4:17.

The mystical work, *The Way of Your Commandments*,[40] explains the hidden symbolism behind each of the Torah's commandments. Starting at the beginning, the book opens with a discussion of the first commandment in the Book of Genesis: "Be fruitful and multiply."[41] The author explains: "There are three partners in the creation of every child: man and woman form the body, and God infuses the soul."[42] It's taught that before a soul descends into a body, it dwells in the presence of God, enjoying its closeness with the Divine.

"Before descending into this world, the soul basked in the radiance of God's Divine Presence....And even if a person lived thousands of years in complete peace and tranquility, living as a king of all kings, lacking absolutely nothing of all of the world's bountiful pleasures, in truth it wouldn't be worth even one moment of pleasure in the lowest levels of the spiritual worlds.... As it is said: 'A single moment of bliss in the World to Come is greater than all of the present world.'"[43]

The fleeting pleasures of this world cannot compare to a glimmer of a moment of pleasure experienced in the afterlife. It's like comparing the pleasure a four year old has when eating chocolate, with the level of pleasure that Einstein felt when discovering the general theory of relativity. But if the soul was enjoying such an intense closeness with God and indescribable pleasure before descending into a body, why did it need to enter this world at all?

---

[40] Written by Menachem Mendel Schneersohn, the 3rd Leader of Lubavitch, also known as the Tzemach Tzedek (1789-1866).

[41] Genesis 1:28.

[42] In connection with this concept of parents partnering with God to create a child, we can learn the great importance Judaism places on honoring one's parents. It is interesting to note that the Ten Commandments were written on two tablets: the first five are in regard to one's relationship with God; the second five are in regard to one's relationship with one's fellow man. But the last commandment of the first tablet between man and God is, "Honor your Father and your mother." How come this is on the list of directives between man and God? Our Sages explain that honoring one's parents is almost akin to honoring God. They are partners in your creation.

[43] Derech Mitzvotecha 1:1.

There is one key advantage to life in this world over the next. In this world, we can create a *real* relationship with God. Before birth, the soul enjoyed a relationship with the Divine like a small child has with his mother. It's a beautiful and pure love that will always be there. But the child hasn't done anything for his mother yet. The soul is like a spectator watching an enjoyable movie. It hasn't yet faced any hurdles or obstacles in its relationship with God. But once the soul enters a body inside the real world, it faces daily struggles in a reality where the spiritual is hidden. Our accomplishments here are earned, and they generate a true pleasure above. A two-sided relationship is being developed. The spiritual level of the soul in the heavenly realms was incredibly lofty, but finite. Our efforts in this world have an infinite effect.

To illustrate the preciousness of good deeds in this world, it's interesting to note that, in Jewish law, one who visits a cemetery must tuck in the *tzitzit* fringes[44] on his shirt so as not to engender jealousy in those who have passed on. They are now incapable of performing commandments on earth.[45] We can now better understand the above teaching: *A single moment of repentance and good deeds in this world is greater than all of the World to Come.*

So, it's true that the material pleasures of this world are as nothing compared to even one moment of spiritual pleasure in the next world. But our souls came down to the finite world for a special purpose: to accomplish something of infinite value.

---

[44] A commandment in the Torah to place a special set of tassels on the fringes of four cornered shirts, as a reminder to fulfill God's commandments.

[45] Shulchan Aruch 23:1.

CHAPTER 4

Visionaries

Abraham—Ten Tests

The Sages teach that God gave Abraham ten tests to see if he was truly devoted to Him. "Our forefather Abraham was tested with ten trials and withstood all of them."[46]

The most well-known tests included leaving his birthplace for an unknown land, circumcising himself at an old age, and his willingness to follow the command to sacrifice his beloved son Isaac (God stopped him as it was only a test). But only briefly mentioned in the *Midrash* is an event that most of us would surely expect to be included as one of the ten tests.

When Abraham first arrives at his belief in one God, he tries to spread this idea to others. His father doesn't appreciate it when Abraham smashes the idols in his shop. So he hands him over to the vicious King Nimrod for judgment of his heretical behavior.[47]

King Nimrod gives young Abraham an ultimatum: Renounce his belief in one God or be killed by fire. He refuses to waver and is thrown

---

[46] Ethics of Our Fathers 5:4. "This demonstrates how beloved Abraham was to God."

[47] These events, described in the Midrash, have been depicted in an animated movie, entitled: *Young Abraham.*

into a fiery furnace. The Midrash teaches that, miraculously, Abraham survives unscathed and runs into hiding.[48]

Why is this incredible story excluded from the tests enumerated in the five books of Moses?

Let's compare the difference between Abraham's encounter with King Nimrod with his other tests. In his father's idol shop, and later when confronted with Nimrod's furnace, Abraham's incredible self-sacrifice is based on his *own feelings* of conviction. However, when he agrees to journey to a foreign land or to perform a circumcision, it's based on God who is *asking* Abraham to do it.

When you do something great for someone, especially when it wasn't asked for, it's certainly special. But it's still an act that's on your terms. When someone asks you for something they need, it's now an act that's on *their* terms. It's admirable when we give of ourselves out of sudden inspiration. But a deeper commitment is shown when we do what's asked of us, especially when we don't feel like it. Here, the deeds are not mortal anymore; they take on a Godly element.[49]

A wife and husband are happily lounging together comfortably. She turns to her husband and asks him for a glass of water. He replies that he would rather stay and be with her. He feels happy spending time with her, and that's great! But she thinks to herself that if he truly loved her, he would help her with what she needs, not what he feels like doing. Real love and devotion mean doing what the other asks of us, not only what we feel like doing or personally think is best, however good our intentions may be. As true as this is in human relationships, it applies as well in our relationship with the Divine. Doing good of our own volition is a noble

---

[48] Bereishit Rabbah, ch. 38.

[49] This is why Abraham waited to circumcise himself only *after* God commanded him to do so, as opposed to all the other commandments that the forefathers knew to perform even before the Torah was given. Abraham knew that he could only be circumcised once, and he understood that the divine power he could draw down *after* God would command him would be much greater than if he performed it based only on his feeling (Avodat Yisroel, p. 19).

pursuit, but doing what we're asked to do by God and our loved ones shows a deeper commitment and connection.

Jacob—Dressed for the Occasion

Abraham and Sarah have a son named Isaac, who marries Rebecca. After waiting many long years for children, Isaac and Rebecca joyfully welcome twin sons into the world, Esau and Jacob. But as the brothers grow, they quickly begin heading in different directions: "And the youths grew up, and Esau was a man who understood hunting, a man of the field, whereas Jacob was a wholesome man, dwelling in tents."[50] Jacob preoccupies himself with learning and character refinement, while Esau ventures into the world to hunt and conquer, often using excessive violence while doing so.

As time passes, Isaac feels his death may soon be approaching. He asks his son Esau to make him a meal, and tells him that upon his return, he will bless him. But Rebecca believes that Jacob is more deserving of Isaac's powerful blessings. She quickly instructs Jacob to impersonate Esau and enter his father's tent with food she will prepare before Esau returns. Because Isaac in his old age has lost his sight, the plan has a chance. To mimic Esau's hairiness, Jacob dresses in fur and enters his father's tent with the prepared meal.

"And Isaac said to Jacob, 'Please come closer, so that I may feel whether you are really my son Esau or not. So Jacob drew near to Isaac his father, and he felt him, and he said:

'The voice is the voice of Jacob, but the hands are the hands of Esau...' And he came closer, and he kissed him, and he smelled the fragrance of his garments, and he blessed him, and he said:

'Behold, the fragrance of my son is like the fragrance of a field which God has blessed!'"[51]

***

---

[50] Genesis 25:27.

[51] Genesis 27:21-27.

Let's examine this strange sequence of events. Why did Isaac want to bless the wicked Esau instead of the righteous Jacob in the first place? Why did Rebecca decide to go against her husband's wishes through trickery instead of directly? What's the meaning of Isaac's words?

The Sages explain that Isaac and Rebecca both had the right intentions and goals to help their sons reach their full potential, differing only in how best to accomplish that.[52] Discussion and explanation on this series of events abound, but let's focus here on one aspect of the story: If the blessings were ultimately meant for Jacob, why did God create such a circumstance where he had to wear a disguise in order to receive them?

The Hassidic masters explain a deeper meaning behind these events. Jacob, the "unblemished one," is a symbol for the soul. Esau, the hunter, is a symbol for the body and physical desire. In order for the soul (*Jacob*) to receive divine blessing (*Isaac's blessing*) to help fulfill its purpose, it needs to descend from the spiritual realms into a body (*Esau's clothing*). To impact the material world, the soul needs a vessel to work within. A soul can't light Shabbat candles, give money to charity, put on *Tefillin*,[53] or cook a meal for a person in need. But hands can. The body is a vehicle the soul needs to succeed in its mission on earth.

While traveling through life in this physical vehicle, we must never forget that we are *Jacob,* even while dressed in *Esau's clothing.* We mustn't lose sight of the original purpose for our excursion into *Esau's clothing*—to elevate the world with spiritual intention.

---

[52] Both parents sensed that their family's ultimate purpose was to refine Esau, who in a cosmic sense symbolizes the animal soul and the material pleasures of this world. Isaac believed that through his lofty blessings he would be able to uplift Esau and reveal his inner potential for righteousness, while Rebecca realized that only through Jacob and his descendants could Esau be rectified. Later in life after they've grown, we see them unify in harmony. But this will only be fully realized in a future time of redemption.

[53] Known in English as, "phylacteries," Tefillin is a commandment for boys over the age of thirteen during prayer to wrap boxes containing specific verses from the Torah on their arm and on their head between the eyes, channeling mind and heart toward a good purpose in a holistic way.

"The voice is the voice of Jacob, but the hands are the hands of Esau."[54] Through the *voice of Jacob*—words of positive speech, prayer, and Torah learning—we can infuse our business dealings and daily activities with the right intention. Even in the clothes of Esau, we must always remember to listen to the voice of Jacob within. But it's only through the *hands of Esau*—action in this world—that the purpose of humanity is achieved. Then we will merit the abundant *blessings of Isaac*, materially and spiritually.

Joseph—Caring in a Dungeon

"Do not be distressed...for having sold me...since it was in order to provide for your needs that God sent me ahead of you.... It was not you who sent me here, but God. He has made me...ruler over all of Egypt."[55]

After years of estrangement from his brothers, Joseph, the second-most powerful person in Egypt, reveals his identity to them in one of the most moving events of the entire Torah.

But how did a teenage slave from Israel find his way to such a lofty position? After near death at the hands of his brothers, Joseph is sold to a caravan of merchants. Upon arrival in Egypt, his moral code is continually tested. His employer's wife perpetually solicits him to enter into an immoral relationship with her, yet he manages to resist her time and again.[56] He stays true to the values taught to him by his father Jacob.[57]

---

[54] When Jacob and Esau were born, the Torah says that when Esau emerged, Jacob's "hand was grasping Esau's heel." The soul must have a hold on the physical in order to uplift it, without becoming consumed by it.

[55] Genesis 45:5-8.

[56] This couldn't have been Joseph's only test with temptation, for it is said that Joseph had such an indescribable beauty that whenever he would walk the streets, women would stop and fight just to catch a glimpse of him.

[57] "All that happened to Jacob happened to Joseph." Our Sages teach us that Joseph and Jacob were extremely close, their connection and destiny intertwined. Both are forced to leave the realm of solitude and holiness to venture into the immoral abyss of ancient Egypt at a very young age. Both have significant dreams, are despised by their brother(s), are exiled from Israel, are lost to their fathers for exactly twenty-two years, and both eventually pass away in Egypt, only to later be buried in Israel.

Joseph knows that his forced descent into Egypt isn't a random occurrence. He understands there's a reason behind the hurdles in his life, including his wrongful arrest and twelve-year imprisonment. After his liberation, he is also aware that his ascent to power with control over the entire Egyptian nation is all part of a greater divine plan. Joseph embraces every situation he is placed in with the intention to better his surroundings. Ultimately, Joseph's plan saves not only the Egyptian people but also the entire world during a great famine. Instead of succumbing to temptations or wallowing in self-pity over the unfair hardships he's endured, Joseph illuminates the darkness around him.

There's a critical moment in Joseph's life that defines his future and the future of the world.

***

One morning, many years into his life as an Egyptian dungeon inmate, Joseph sees two dejected prisoners sitting on their own. He walks over to them with a friendly smile.

"Why are your faces sad today?"[58]

The Pharaoh's butler and baker then describe to Joseph the nightmares they had experienced the night before, and Joseph interprets them. Consistent with his interpretation, the butler is soon freed, and upon hearing the Pharaoh complain of his own nightmare, he begrudgingly admits that he met a Hebrew slave with a talent for dream interpretation. Joseph interprets the Pharaoh's dreams to mean that seven years of great famine will soon strike Egypt and that they must prepare immediately by storing the surplus grain. The Pharaoh is impressed and appoints Joseph to second in command of Egypt, in charge of planning for the impending disaster. Joseph begins to store grain immediately, which eventually feeds the entire starving world during the years of famine.

***

---

[58] Genesis 40:7.

Let's take a deeper look at the life of Joseph. At a young age, his mother Rachel dies. After years of being hated by his brothers and nearly murdered, Joseph is sold as a slave and shipped to a foreign land. Soon, he's framed for a crime he never committed, and finds himself alone in a dungeon indefinitely, with no one who cares if he lives or dies.

At this stage of his life, depression and self-absorption would be the most understandable reactions Joseph could have. Yet all that concerns Joseph when he sees two sad-looking prisoners is how he can help them. *At this moment, in this place I'm in, how can I make a difference?* Joseph understood that every soul is important and every action we take can make a crucial difference, regardless of how bleak our circumstances may be. Our life's mission is vital to the world. "Save a life, and you've saved a world."[59]

Joseph had an unimaginable sensitivity and caring nature, and he also understood that every situation happens for a reason. He had to try and make any difference he could, even in a dungeon. Because of this one caring action in the darkest of places, Joseph ends up saving the entire world! Instead of only focusing on global conflict resolution, what if each of us took a moment to ask the dejected coworker near our desk how she's feeling?

***

A man was walking on a beach when he noticed a child picking something up and gently throwing it into the ocean. Approaching the boy, he asked: "What are you doing there, son?"

The boy replied: "I'm throwing starfish back into the ocean. The surf is up and the tide is going out. If I don't throw them back, they'll die!"

---

[59] Sanhedrin 37a, explains that God created only one human being and not many at the beginning of creation to show the immense value of each life: "Whoever destroys a single life is as guilty as though he had destroyed the entire world; and whoever rescues a single life earns as much merit as though he had rescued the entire world." One person is as valuable as an entire world.

"Son," the man said with exasperation as he scanned the beach, "don't you realize there are miles and miles of land and thousands of starfish? You can't possibly make a difference here!"

After listening politely, the boy bent down and picked up another starfish. Smiling, he threw the starfish into the surf and replied: "It made a difference to that one."

Joseph and Benjamin—The Neck

One of the most dramatic events in the Torah occurs when Joseph, viceroy of Egypt, reveals his true identity to his stunned brothers, after more than two decades apart.

"Joseph fell upon his brother Benjamin's neck and wept, and Benjamin wept upon his neck."[60]

Rashi comments: "Joseph wept for the two temples that would be built in Benjamin's territory in Israel and that would later be destroyed. And Benjamin wept for the Tabernacle in Shiloh, Joseph's territory, which would be destroyed."

Why did they weep for the destruction of the Temple in their brother's territory but not for the destruction in their own?

This moment between Joseph and Benjamin is a powerful lesson for how to approach life's struggles. When tough times befall us, we mustn't give up and wallow in self-pity. The proper response is to summon our inner strength and take steps to fix the situation. But when it comes to the misfortune of others, we need to empathize with them and feel their pain. Joseph and Benjamin were willing to confront their own challenges. But the pain their brother felt was intolerable to them. Let's work on having trust and being resilient in the face of our own challenges, while not expecting that of others, always showing compassion toward others who are struggling.

---

[60] Genesis 45:14.

Moses—Appreciation

"God said to Moses: 'Say to Aaron, Take your staff and stretch out your hand over the waters of Egypt...and they shall become blood.'"[61]

"Take your staff and strike the dust of the earth; and it will turn into lice throughout the whole land of Egypt."[62]

***

The Pharaoh of Egypt, fearing a potential future uprising, decrees that every newborn male be thrown into the Nile River and drowned. When Yoheved gives birth to Moses, she places him in a secure basket and floats it along the river in hopes of escaping the clutches of the Egyptian authorities. Thankfully, the basket is found by Pharaoh's very own daughter, Batya,[63] who saves the boy and decides to raise him as her own. Baby Moses refuses to be nursed by the Egyptian nurse maids, so Yoheved the Israelite is called in to help. She nurses and raises her son, teaching him of his heritage and people, before he is given back into Batya's care in the palace.

One day, years later, Moses walks out of the palace and sees an Egyptian taskmaster brutally beating a Hebrew slave. Unable to tolerate such injustice, Moses utters a secret name of God, instantly killing the Egyptian, whom he hides in the sand. The Pharaoh is enraged when he hears of this and decrees death upon his adopted grandson. So Moses flees, only to return years later upon God's command to liberate his people. When the Pharaoh scoffs at this cheeky request, God begins the ten plagues that ultimately lead to the freedom of the Jewish people.

***

---

[61] Exodus 7:19. The Hassidic Masters teach a lesson we can take from the plague of water turning into blood: Water is cold; blood is warm—we must strive to turn our *cold* demeanors spiritually into a *warm* excitement.

[62] Exodus 8:12.

[63] *Batya* means "daughter of God." She is so named in honor of her saving one of God's children.

39

Strangely, God commands Moses to execute only the last seven plagues while his brother Aaron is asked to execute the first three, which includes the water turning into blood and the frog and lice infestations. Why was Moses excluded from the first three?

The *Midrash* explains: "Since the river protected Moses when he was thrown into it, he couldn't execute the plague of water into blood, or the frogs which came up from the river waters."[64] Regarding the plague of lice, it's taught: "It was not fitting that the plague of dust be struck by Moses because it protected him when he killed the Egyptian and hid him in the sand, so it was instead struck by Aaron."[65]

This isn't an isolated example of the Torah teaching the importance of gratitude to a nonhuman. One of the great commentators on the Talmud teaches that the reason we cover the two *hallah* loaves on the Sabbath while covering the wine, is because we do not want to embarrass the bread. It would be disrespectful to the bread were it to be uncovered, since every day we make a blessing over the bread first, and only afterward do we bless the wine. But on the Sabbath, we start with the wine.[66] Numerous laws were instituted to treat animals with compassion and respect, including the commandment to feed your animals before feeding yourself.[67]

If Torah law emphasizes gratitude, respect, and sensitivity even toward inanimate matter, how much more so must this apply to the living beings around us?

---

[64] Midrash Shemot Rabbah 9:10.

[65] Rashi, Exodus 8:12.

[66] Mordechai, Perek Arvei Pesachim.

[67] Berachot 40a on Deuteronomy 11:15.

Unlike the river and earth that aided Moses, human beings who help and show kindness toward us do so out of free choice.[68] How often do we receive good from others, but choose to focus on what we haven't been given?

"Rabbi Elazar, son of Shamua, said: 'The honor of your student should be as dear to you as your own. The honor of your colleague should be as the awe of your teacher. And the awe of your teacher should be as the awe of Heaven.'"[69]

The Talmud states: "A person should not cast stones into the well from which he has drunk."[70] It's often toward those that we owe the most gratitude that we show the least. Who knows how many times we will still have the chance to show our gratitude?

Let us make a greater effort to acknowledge and express our appreciation to our loved ones while showing respect to all forms of life.[71]

---

[68] The biggest emphasis placed by the Torah on displaying gratitude is in regard to our parents. The Rabbis add that this is a deed that increases longevity of life: "These matters are those that a man eats their fruits in this world and their principal is retained for him in the World to Come. And these are they: Honoring one's father and mother..." (Shabbat 127a). Regarding the question of why honoring one's parents is one of the first five of the Ten Commandments, which are supposed to be laws between man and God only, the Rabbis teach: "There are three partners in a person's creation: The Holy One, blessed be He, the father, and the mother" (Niddah 31a).

[69] Ethics of Our Fathers 4:15.

[70] Baba Kama 92b.

[71] Rabbi Yoseph Yitzchak Schneerson writes in his diary, that as a child he was once walking in the forest with his father, the holy Rebbe Rashab. He saw a leaf and without thinking, tore it off and threw it to the ground. His father turned to him: "How can one be so callous towards a creation of God? This leaf was created by the Almighty for a specific purpose, and is imbued with a divine life force. It has a body, and it has its life. In what way is the 'I' of this leaf inferior to yours?"

Rabbi Akiva—A Fish in Water

There was a time in Israel under Roman occupation when teaching Torah was a capital offense. The great Rabbi Akiva[72] wasn't intimidated by the threat of death and persisted in teaching Torah, especially to children. His colleagues tried to reason with him.

"Akiva, if you continue, you'll surely be killed. Those you teach might be killed as well. But if you stop, at least there's a chance of survival!"

Rabbi Akiva replied with a parable.

***

There was once a fox resting by a river. Peering into the water, the fox saw a group of worried-looking fish.

"What's the problem?" asked the fox.

The fish answered: "There are fishermen waiting to catch us by the edge of the river!"

"OK," said the fox after some thought. "I have a plan. Jump on my back and I'll secretly usher you to the other end of the river. When we've passed the fishermen, I'll drop you back in."

The fish burst into laughter. "We thought you foxes were sly. If we leave the water, we'll perish for sure since we can't survive without water! But if we stay in the water, at least we have a chance at survival."[73]

***

---

[72] Rabbi Akiva was a farmer who was ignorant of Judaism until the age of 40. One day, he saw drops of water dripping on a large boulder. Over many years, the constant dripping had made an indent in the hard rock. He realized at that moment that Torah could penetrate his mind, even as unlearned as he was, if only he dedicated himself with constant effort to learning it. After twenty-four years of learning, he returned home as the greatest sage of his generation, and is renowned today as one of the wisest to have ever lived. When you set your mind toward achieving a goal, anything is possible.

[73] Berachot 61b.

Rabbi Akiva explained that the divine wisdom of the Torah is for us like water is for a fish. It's our spiritual life force and a vital guiding light during times of darkness, enabling us to thrive in any environment.

In the twenty-first-century Western world, unlike in generations past, the tests we face are often less of a physical nature and more of a spiritual nature. The "foxes" of today are very enticing. They beckon us to leave our water— our identity and values— to join them for a life of freedom on land. Why immerse ourselves in spirituality and Torah values if we'll miss out on all the fun that life on land has to offer?

Look at a fish that leaves its environment. It appears to be having a great time, flopping and dancing around on dry land. But in reality, the fish is dying. Just as our bodies need to be taken care of, our souls require equal nourishment. A life of materialism without greater meaning can lead to a feeling of existential angst. Outer laughter can hide an inner depression; the transient highs of substance abuse mask an inner yearning for greater meaning in life.[74]

The prophet Isaiah taught: "All who are thirsty, go to water."[75] While focused on our daily pursuits and goals, it's vital we sustain our souls by staying connected to our life force. Daily doses of Torah wisdom help us to thrive and navigate the hurdles of life. Like water for fish, learning Torah wisdom is indispensable to our spiritual survival.

Baal Shem Tov—A Lesson in Warmth

It was a particularly difficult time in Jewish History. The *Chmielnicki massacres* of 1648-1649 had recently killed between 100,000 and 500,000 Jews. Many were understandably disheartened and cold toward religion, God, and life itself. In 1698, a man named Israel was born, later known universally as the Baal Shem Tov—"Master of a good name." He dedicated his life to

---

[74] A study of this human need for purpose can be examined further in renowned psychiatrist and Holocaust survivor Viktor Frankl's memoir, *Man's Search for Meaning*.

[75] Isaiah 55:1.

inspiring hearts and minds, emphasizing a renewed joy, optimism, and trust in divine providence. He explained that the simple cries to heaven of the unlearned are as beloved by God as the most in-depth study of the wisest of scholars. Regardless of spiritual standing, God's love is absolute, like a mother's love for her newborn child.

The Baal Shem Tov taught that we can learn a lesson from everything we see.

***

Once, the Baal Shem Tov and his holy group of disciples were journeying through a forest. As they entered a clearing, they saw a frozen lake. On the ice was carved an idolatrous image.

"Rabbi!" exclaimed his students. "You've always taught us that everything we see and experience is a lesson in life and in the service of God. But what could possibly be the purpose of God showing us this?"

The Baal Shem Tov paused for a moment. Turning to his students, he said:

"Why are you able to see such an image on water?"

"Because the water is frozen," they answered.

"So, if the water were warmed and the ice melted, would this image be able to exist?"

The students understood the message.

***

The Baal Shem Tov taught that our relationship with God needs to be vibrant, infused with warmth and energy. When one's relationship with the Divine is cold, lacking joy and excitement, it can lead to a downward spiritual spiral. In those moments when we feel stagnant and cold, we can be warmed by the knowledge that every effort we make to grow and connect above is incredibly precious, like a toddler attempting to walk toward the loving embrace of his mother. The effort alone is cherished more than we can possibly imagine.

Reb Zusha—Holy Breakfast

In mid-eighteenth-century Eastern Europe, in the village of Hanipol, there lived a beloved sage, known far and wide as Reb Zusha. Every morning he would arise well before dawn, study for a while, and then head to the local synagogue to recite his morning prayers with great devotion. Afterward, he would return home, enter his room, and open his window. Lifting his eyes toward the heavens, he would call out:

"Master of the Universe, Zusha is hungry and needs something to eat!"

Each day, his attendant would wait until he heard this appeal, and would then bring in his breakfast.

One morning, the attendant thought to himself: "Why doesn't Reb Zusha ask me directly for his meal? Who does he think he's fooling by calling out to God when he knows perfectly well that it is I who brings him his food every day?"

He decided that the next morning he would not bring in a meal when the sage called out. He eagerly anticipated how Reb Zusha would react when he didn't receive his meal.

The next morning, Reb Zusha awoke early as usual. It had rained all night, and the streets of Hanipol had turned into rivers of mud. In order to get from one side of the street to the other, Reb Zusha had to cross on narrow planks that were laid across the flowing mud.

As he was crossing the planks in the direction of the synagogue, a man from out of town was coming toward him from the other side. The humble sage had a disheveled appearance, was gaunt and dressed in rags. Seeing what looked like a beggar, the stranger, with a hearty laugh, jumped up and down on the plank causing Reb Zusha to tumble into the mud. Without a word, he picked himself up from the mud and continued on his way to the synagogue, while the stranger sauntered off toward the local tavern with a bellowing laugh.

When he arrived at the tavern, the bartender looked at him curiously.

"Sir, why are you so happy at such an early hour this morning?"

The man bragged to the bartender about his amusing prank. But the bartender wasn't so quick to laugh. He asked the guest to describe the appearance of this beggar whom he had catapulted into the mud, and upon hearing his description, he cried out in anguish.

"Do you know what you've done!? That was no ordinary beggar; that was the great Reb Zusha!"

By this time the guest had stopped laughing, for Reb Zusha was known to all as a holy man and miracle worker.

Trembling, he stammered: "What am I going to do!?"

"Don't worry," said the bartender, as he regained his composure. "I have an idea. Reb Zusha spends many hours every morning in prayer. When he returns home, he opens his window, thrusts his head out, and calls toward the heavens for food. I'll quickly prepare some cakes and schnapps for you to bring to him, and when you hear him call out, enter immediately with your gift and beg his forgiveness."

As usual, after completing his morning prayers, Reb Zusha walked to his window and called out to the heavens, asking the Master of the Universe for a morsel of food.

With a smirk, Reb Zusha's attendant defiantly stood in his place.

"Let his Master of the Universe bring him his cake this morning!"

Suddenly the front door burst open, and a man holding a large plate of cakes and drinks ran past the bewildered attendant into Reb Zusha's room. Placing the tray on the table, he fell to the floor in grief, begging for forgiveness. The attendant then understood. It truly was the Master of the Universe who brought Reb Zusha his breakfast every morning.

***

A businessman was running late to an important business meeting. Driving through the large parking lot, he desperately searched for an open space, but to no avail. His panicked thoughts began moving heavenward.

"God, if you help me find a parking space, I will donate to charity ten percent of whatever profits I accrue from this deal."

As he continued to circle the parking lot, with mounting panic, the amount he declared he would donate increased rapidly until it reached fifty percent. Two minutes

46

before the meeting, a car pulled out right in front of the building's entrance! Excitedly, the man pulled in, and jumped out of his car.

"Don't worry God, I found a space!"

***

Whether we credit our boss for the checks we receive, or "the Universe" for our blessings, everything in our lives comes from a higher source. There are many natural conduits for these blessings, but it's important to remember their true source. The bulb may shine light, but the electric current comes from the power station. Our hard work, networking, and intelligence are all useful tools to lead a successful business life. But all of our talents and efforts are simply vessels for divine blessings. Where you succeed, many with equal skill and great effort fail. If we put forth our maximum effort and create a vessel for blessing, we can be calm, mindful that the end result comes from God and will always be for the best.

CHAPTER 5

Relationships

The Deck of Cards

Mendel Futerfas, fondly known as Reb Mendel, was someone who inspired all who met him. He suffered great hardship in his life because of his self-sacrifice to teach children Judaism in Communist Russia, something that was strictly forbidden. This cost him fourteen years of hard labor in the Siberian Gulags. After completing his prison term, he moved to Israel and continued teaching in schools until his passing in 1995.

Reb Mendel often said that every circumstance in which he found himself provided a lesson for life he could learn from.

A student of his once recounted the following story he heard directly from him.

***

One night in the labor camps, I was resting in a room I shared with other prisoners.[76] *They were having a great time playing cards, a forbidden activity in the Gulags. All of a sudden we heard footsteps, and in stormed one of the officers.*

"Where are the cards?" yelled the officer.

"I know you're playing cards, and I'm going to catch you."

---

[76] The Russian labor camps (Gulags) housed any violators of law in the eyes of the government, from true criminals to those who merely violated intellectual and religious ordinances.

I looked and saw that the cards had disappeared. Glancing around the room and seeing nothing, the officer stormed out in a rage. As soon as he was gone, the cards were right back on the table, and the game continued as before. After a few minutes, the door again slammed open. This time the officer brought others with him, and they searched every prisoner, turning over tables and chairs, looking everywhere for the illegal cards. I was amazed at how the players had hidden the cards so well. After fifteen minutes, the officers left, exasperated. When the cards were placed back on the table, I pleaded with the players to reveal the amazing trick of hiding the cards.

Initially they refused, but eventually the card dealer told me that they were thieves by trade and swift with their hands. Whenever the officer entered, he would take the deck and secretly place it into the officer's pocket.

"It's the only place he never thinks to check."

Later that night, I thought about this episode. What lesson could I learn from this? I soon realized that when there's trouble in a relationship, we so often busy ourselves checking for the problem in the other's "pockets" that we forget to check our own. This may be where the real issue is to be found.

***

Generally, when friction occurs in any relationship, our natural reaction is to find blame in the other person. *If only he was like this or she acted like that, everything would be so much smoother.* But what if part of the problem lies with us?[77] Drastically changing those around us is also quite difficult, if not near impossible. We do, however, have the power to change ourselves.

---

[77] Rabbi Israel Salanter, founder of the *Mussar* movement—Jewish ethical mindfulness—once said: "When I was young, I wanted to change the world. I found this difficult and decided to focus instead on changing my country. When I found I couldn't accomplish even that, I began to focus on my city. When I couldn't change my town, I worked to change my family. Now as an older man, I've realized that I should primarily focus on changing myself, and even that is incredibly challenging. If I had first started on changing myself, I may have in turn had an impact on my family, city, country, and ultimately the world." Yes we can change the world, but we must focus on working on ourselves as well, aware of the ripple effect our growth can have on the world around us.

This inward focus on change can also cause a positive influence of change in those around us.

***

Centuries ago, a disgruntled man approached his Rabbi about seeking a divorce.

"Rabbi, my wife doesn't cook, clean, or manage the duties of our home like the others do!"

"I completely understand," sympathized the Rabbi. "But this week, I want you to try something strange for me. I want you to clean the dishes, cook the meals, and do the laundry yourself."

Out of respect for his Rabbi, the confused man did as he was told. A week later, he came running to his Rabbi.

"Rabbi, you won't believe what happened!" he said. "Soon after my wife saw me cleaning and cooking, she joined in to help, and at one point, she even moved me out of the way to take over!"

***

Beside the fact that spouses should help each other, we see that when we worry less about what others are doing for us, and focus more on how we can improve, we may be surprised at how our relationships improve. The Hebrew term for "love" is connected to the word "give."[78] Through focusing on how we can give and improve the quality of life of another, our relationship and feelings of love will thrive.

Marriage

Is getting married a holy act?

Many religious systems frown upon intimacy and relationships as weaknesses of the human condition, believing it leads to sin and lust. They argue it's wiser to shun physicality completely and focus solely on spiritual matters.

---

[78] *Ahava* (love) and *hav* (give/offer).

A loving relationship is arguably the most powerful aspect of a human's life. These relationships have the potential to be the most richly rewarding experiences human beings have, or the most tumultuous and heartbreaking.

To find the true nature of anything, we must inspect its Hebrew name. *Marriage* in Hebrew is *kiddushin*—to sanctify. An intimate relationship can be a lofty spiritual experience that gets to the core of what our purpose is on earth.

We have to engage with the physical world, elevating and refining our human experiences to a higher plane. Every holiday in Judaism, including a wedding, is sanctified over a cup of wine, known as *kiddush*. A spiritual occasion is purposely honored with an intoxicating substance that can lead to an extremely elevated or debased state.[79] Everything in our world is a mixture of good and bad, and either can be highlighted, depending on our intention. The ultimate challenge of life is to engage the world without being pulled down and degraded, elevating and bringing out the good in all that we encounter.

There is no greater fusion of the physical and spiritual than in the union of male and female. Rather than shun intimacy, we sanctify it with purpose and meaning. Because the deepest potential for holiness is found here, it's not by chance that this is one of the most powerful of human experiences. This connection of two opposites contains the potential for creating a greater life of significance together than is possible on one's own. This union can even produce the most incredible feat of all: a new life.

---

[79] The prominence of wine on these days isn't accidental. Nearly every physical thing deteriorates over time, from our bodies to the food we eat. Wine, however, is special in that it improves over time. Wine symbolizes matters of the spirit, where wisdom and character growth only improve in value over time, and thus is the most appropriate item for a time where the spiritual is appreciated and the physical and spiritual are to join together. This is why the elderly are so valued, for while they may be less adept at lifting weights, in the areas that matter most, like wisdom, they have only increased in value.

Everything in the spiritual world is directly mirrored in the physical. Just as the union of male and female creates physical life, the mystics teach that in the supernal worlds, masculine and feminine divine energies unite to create spiritual worlds. How incredible it is that we are able to mimic God in our relationships and partner with Him in creating life![80]

A Bouquet of Flowers

Joe, who is newly married, walks through a busy mall on a Friday afternoon. As he texts on his cell phone, he spots a florist shop full of bouquets of beautiful flowers. Knowing his wife's love for flowers, especially daisies, Joe walks in and buys their most expensive arrangement and hurries home to his wife.

Joe might have any one of four motives for wanting to buy these daisies:

Joe loves a good dinner and knows that when his wife receives these flowers, she will be in such good spirits that she will cook him an extra special dish. This is the lowest motive.

Joe knows that by making his wife happy, this will create a pleasant environment in their home.

Joe wants to be a good husband who shows he cares.

Joe wants to buy these flowers because he knows that his wife will enjoy them.

Joe's first three motives have something in common—they have nothing to do with his wife's feelings. His purchase benefits his life or self esteem in some way. These four motives found in human relationships, are also in our relationship with God. Doing something in order to

---

[80] "There are three partners in a person, the Holy One blessed be He, his father and his mother. His father supplies the white substance out of which are formed the child's bones, sinews, nails, the brain in his head and the white in his eye; his mother supplies the red substance out of which is formed his skin, flesh, hair, blood, and the black of his eye; and the Holy One, blessed be He, gives him the spirit and the breath, beauty of features, eyesight, the power of hearing and the ability to speak and to walk, understanding and discernment" (Niddah 31a).

receive a better dinner is like serving God so that we will be blessed with material abundance.

Buying flowers to create peace in the home is akin to serving God in order to merit a pleasant afterlife. This motive is loftier than wanting a better dinner, but it's still self-serving. A more refined level is the desire to be a good husband; that is, doing good deeds in order to refine our characters and become better people.

All of these motives are positive and productive, because most importantly, they lead us to do the right thing. Joe bought the flowers and brightened his wife's day. The good deed was done.[81] However, one's true love for another is not only exemplified by an action, but by the intention behind it. The fourth motive, buying the flowers because *she* likes them, is the highest level. This is like serving God simply because of the pleasure it brings Him.

Judaism teaches that the highest form of giving is when it's focused on the needs of the other. Try to do acts of kindness for others, not to get something in return but simply because it benefits them. We too can serve God simply because of the pleasure it brings Him and not for the reward we will receive in return.

Caring for Another

Zev Greenglass was a saintly kabbalist who lived in Montreal, Canada. He once recounted an experience that had a profound impact on him during his adolescence.

---

[81] As crucial as our intentions are, it's important not to forget the power behind a simple action: *Rabbi Elazar ben Azariah used to say: Anyone whose wisdom exceeds his good deeds, to what is he similar? To a tree whose branches are many and whose roots are few; then the wind will come and uproot it and turn it over...But one whose deeds exceed his wisdom, to what is he similar? To a tree whose branches are few and whose roots are many; even if all the winds in the world come and blow against it, they will not move it from its place* (Ethics of our Fathers, 3:22). As the Lubavitcher Rebbe constantly taught: *Ha'maaseh hu ha'ikar* —"Action is the main thing."

***

I was traveling through a town in my native Russia and needed a place to stay for the night. I found a school of Torah learning and asked a student if there was a room available for the night.

"No problem," he told me. "My roommate is away at a wedding. You can take his bed."

I was led, exhausted, to his room and went straight to sleep.

In the middle of the night, I woke up to use the restroom. As I arose, I saw a peculiar sight. On the floor, fast asleep, was the boy who had offered me his roommate's bed.

I was a complete stranger to him, but knowing I needed a place to rest, he had given his bed to me and made up a story about his roommate being away so I wouldn't refuse. When I awoke early the next morning, the boy was gone. He knew I would have felt bad taking his bed.

This selfless act of kindness changed my life.

***

To genuinely care for the well-being of others isn't always easy. Even though the Torah states, "Love your fellow as you love yourself,"[82] how can we truly feel the same care for a stranger as we do for ourselves?[83]

---

[82] Leviticus 19:18.

[83] Hillel the Elder was asked to explain the entire Torah in one teaching. He replied, "What is hateful to you, do not do to your neighbor: that is the whole Torah, the rest is commentary; now go and learn it." Hassidic teachings explain that if we have a bad character trait such as a quick temper, we generally don't let that action define us. We attribute our character deficiencies to situational mishaps. "That person kept pushing my buttons" or "I didn't really mean it." We know that we aren't bad at the core of our being. We have an intrinsic love, patience, and understanding of ourselves that create a sense of empathy for our mistakes. But if someone else highlights a mistake of ours without looking at the whole picture of who we are, we become hurt and angry. This is what Hillel meant when he taught: "What is hateful to you, do not do to another." Just as you hate when someone defines you by your one bad action without judging you as a whole person, don't do that to another. Just as your self-love overshadows your mistakes, arouse a love and compassion for other people that will cloud over their mistakes. We are not speaking here about abusive relationships.

If you look up from earth at the stars, hundreds of light-years away, each star looks the same as all the others. But if you were able to zoom in and take a closer look at each individual star, you would see the special, distinct quality each star possesses. This is also true of every person we meet. At first glance, we may not see anything special. But if we took a moment to get to know people better, hearing their hopes, dreams, passions and insecurities, we might find an area of connection and see an area where they uniquely shine.

By taking the time to see others beyond the superficial layer they present to the outside world, we can fulfill this vital principle of loving one another.

A Parent's Love

No love compares to the love parents have for their children. This love has deep spiritual roots, directly stemming from God's love for His children.[84] The love a mother feels for her newborn in her arms, is only a glimmer of the love God feels for each of us. The *Baal Shem Tov* likens God to a childless parent who, in her old age, is finally blessed with an only child. It's impossible to put into words how precious this child is to her.

If we meditate on this relationship we have with God, instead of a powerful, judgmental being, there emerges a feeling, loving giver whose only desire is to have a close relationship with His child. When a woman conceives a new life, it develops within her womb and is sustained through her being. After birth, this helpless child survives and is nurtured from the mother's loving beneficence. Children can never fully comprehend the

---

[84] The verse, "And God created Adam in His image" (Genesis 1:27), encompasses every aspect of the human being. The instinctual love parents feel for their child stems directly from God's love for His children. The same applies to all relationships. They are rooted in the various facets of our relationship with the divine.

love of their mothers. This incredible love is rooted in a divine love on an infinitely deeper level.

As a child grows up and matures, the parents still have that same great love, no matter how tumultuous the teenage years become. But now, that intrinsic love is layered with reason and understanding. *I love how thoughtful my daughter is when she includes her friends in events. My son has such a big heart and takes good care of his little sister.* Young children grow and develop their characters.

Spiritually, we too must grow and develop our minds and emotional maturity. We can't stay with the same perspective we had of God and what life is about, as we had as children. But at the same time, we must never think that the intrinsic love our divine parent has for us is hidden. A parent's love transcends any positive traits or flaws their child may have developed.

As we grow into thoughtful adults with complex lives, we must always remember that God's essential love for us is unconditional and, while proud of our accomplishments, will always have that essential love that transcends any appreciation He has for our accomplishments.[85]

A Divine Kiss

The Talmud teaches that the Temple in Jerusalem was a place where "heaven and earth kiss."[86] The Sages were never frivolous with their words, simply employing a colorful use of language. The bond between humanity and God was intimately expressed in that location.

A person's mouth is the ultimate vehicle for expression and bonding. A kiss bonds two people, as does speaking in conversation. The mouth also serves as a connector through eating, uniting the soul and body. Without food and drink, the soul would simply leave and the body would expire.

---

[85] See Likkutei Sichot, Vol. 21, Exodus.

[86] Baba Batra 74a. The Malbim on Genesis 28:17: "Jacob understood that this place was the site of the future Temple... for the Temple is the ladder, whereby heaven and earth kiss each other."

The Temple was an interface, uniting God with the world. As a vehicle of connection, the three activities of the mouth occurred here as well. *Kissing* was represented by the intimate connection between God and humanity, as seen in the *Holy of Holies* where the *Ark of the Covenant* was housed. There were two golden cherubs above the base of the ark— one shaped like a female child's face and one like a male child's face— which symbolized the relationship between God and the people. When the relationship was harmonious, the angelic cherubs would face each other in an embrace. When the relationship had been weakened through immoral action, the cherubs would turn their backs to each other.[87] On Yom Kippur, the holiest day of the year, the *Kohen Gadol* would open up the inner curtains to the Holy of Holies so that all the people could see the cherubs in embrace.

Speech occurred there as well. During the journeys in the desert, the Torah describes how God would communicate with the Jewish nation through *speaking* to Moses from the Holy of Holies. A voice would emanate from above the ark between the two golden cherubs.

Eating was symbolized by the daily sacrifices. The human being is a microcosm of the universe.[88] Through food, the soul attaches itself to the body and gives it vitality. So, too the soul of the world (God's presence) vitalized the world through the daily sacrifices. Today, our *speech* through daily prayer has been substituted for the sacrifices,[89] drawing down God's divine energy into the world.[90]

When the Temple was destroyed, the victors took the spoils, and dragged the golden cherubs through the streets. At this low point in Jewish

---

[87] Baba Batra 99a.

[88] Ibn Ezra on Exodus 25:40. "The heavens are the head of humankind, the sun and the moon are the eyes, and the stars are the hair on the head" (Otzar HaMidrashim). The majority of earth is made up of water, as is the human body.

[89] Berachot 26b. Shulchan Aruch HaRav 98:4.

[90] The term for "blessing" in Hebrew is *berachah*, whose literal translation is, "to draw down." See Genesis 24:11.

history, the Talmud relays that the cherubs were seen to still be in a loving embrace.[91] The message was clear: Our connection with God survives any sin and the bleakest points of exile, and will be made fully manifest in the time of redemption, when the third and final Temple will be rebuilt.

---

[91] Yoma 54a-b.

CHAPTER 6

Holy Days

The Sabbath and Holidays—Being Present

"And the heavens and the earth were completed...And God completed on the seventh day His work which He had done, and He rested on the seventh day...And God blessed the seventh day, and sanctified it."[92]

"Six days shall work be done, but the seventh day shall be holy."[93]

"I have a wonderful present in my Treasure House and its name is Shabbat."[94]

What is the point of the Sabbath? What's so special about its message that necessitates a full day of rest for an entire day every week? Throughout the ages, much was sacrificed to uphold the Sabbath, known in Hebrew as *Shabbat*. Some Jewish immigrants to the United States in the early 20th century used to work fifty-two jobs a year. Every week they refused to work on Saturday and lost their jobs as a result. On Shabbat, we unplug from workday activities and technology, focusing on family and personal spiritual growth. Is it worth risking one's livelihood just to become a hippie for a day, disconnected from the world?

---

[92] Genesis 1:31-2:3.

[93] Exodus 31:15, Exodus 35:2, Leviticus 23:3.

[94] God speaking to Moses (Shabbat 10b).

Shabbat is more than a pleasant respite from work; it is vital to the inner health of our personal and family lives. Now more than ever, we feel restless as we're pulled in every direction with work, family, school, and daily responsibilities.[95] There's precious little time left to develop deeper relationships with our loved ones, communicating and listening without distraction.

This applies to the relationship we have with ourselves as well. When do you take time out of your day to reflect on your life and understand your inner self; the direction you are heading and the person you want to become? We strive for six days of the week to affect the world. Shabbat is an oasis in time where we stop to appreciate the journey of life, meditating on how far we've come. We take time to marvel at the world around us and simply enjoy the present moment. When Shabbat concludes, we start the new week mentally and emotionally rejuvenated, equipped to face whatever may come our way in the week ahead.

The translation of *Shabbat* as "a day of rest" can be misleading. According to Jewish law, there is no problem on the Sabbath if someone wants to carry a heavy couch up a flight of stairs. However, lighting a match or turning the ignition to one's car, while effortless, is prohibited.[96] Surely it's more restful to drive than to walk?

The concept of *Shabbat* is first mentioned in the Book of Genesis. After completing creation, the text says *vayishbot*—God rested. A more accurate translation is: "And He ceased." God hadn't tired from forming the universe. Rather, He ceased to innovate, preferring to delight in what He had already created. On the seventh day, we, too cease creating anew. It's a time for *being*. Don't be scared to quiet the outside world for a

---

[95] In an interview with *Cosmopolitan*, musician Katy Perry remarked: "I wish there was something like Shabbat... Something like this would be great for our minds... I think it's going to be really difficult for our focus and our attention spans moving forward. So I'd love if the world implemented an actual day of real rest" (Carly Cardellino, *Cosmopolitan*, May 2, 2016).

[96] There are thirty-nine labors prohibited on Shabbat derived from the laws performed in the Temple of Jerusalem, including the igniting of a flame.

little bit and find out more about yourself. On this day we move from involvement in the outer world to a focus on our inner world of personal growth and reflection. Going 100 mph toward success in a certain area of life is only worthwhile if you're headed in the right direction. When describing Shabbat later in the Torah, the verse says that after God ceased work, *vayinafash*, which literally means "soul."[97] This is a special time to focus on becoming in tune with your soul.[98]

"Six days you shall work." During the week, we actualize our creative potential by working within the world ethically and morally.[99] We don't shun work and are supposed to immerse ourselves in the world, while elevating all we come in contact with.[100]

But like a painter in the midst of working on a masterpiece, we all need to periodically step back from our work and reflect on the progress we've made with an eye to the future. We can then delve back into our work with renewed focus and energy. In the words of famed author Herman Wouk: "(Shabbat is) a retreat into restorative magic."

Before and After the Sabbath - Garments of Light

What changed after Adam and Eve ate from the *tree of knowledge*?[101] Before this act, the mystics describe that the soul and body fused together seamlessly; the soul illuminated an almost transparent body. Their bodies were *Kotenot Or*—garments of light. Unlike today, their bodies did not hide

---

[97] Exodus 31:17.

[98] We receive an extra soul on Shabbat (Taanit 27b).

[99] The Sages teach that we are asked three questions in the next world, the first being: Did you deal in business honestly?

[100] "God desired to have a dwelling place in the lower realms" (Midrash Tanchuma Naso, 16).

[101] Based on the teachings of Rabbi Akiva Tatz.

their souls, but revealed them.[102] They wore no clothes because there was no reason to feel any shame.

Why would nakedness cause a feeling of shame? Isn't it natural to be unclothed like Adam and Eve were? The shame stems from a false representation. We have an inner awareness that we contain an angelic being—a soul—inside an animalistic body that others see. *They're not seeing the real me!* This dichotomy between the two is difficult to handle. When we see another person, what are we seeing? A body made of flesh. Maybe after spending a while with someone and reflecting, can we notice and connect with another's true self inside.

We clothe our bodies to cover this dichotomy of the outer body and hidden soul. But we do so in a way that demonstrates the dignity of the true self inside. The garments of a king and queen not only hide their bodies beneath, they also reveal their royalty.[103] While Judaism encourages men and women to dress modestly, there was never any suggestion to cover one's face. The word for "face" in Hebrew is *panim,* connected to the word *p'nim*—inner/internal. Emotions are most expressed in the face, an area that displays some of the inner spiritual being behind it.

Before eating from the tree of knowledge, if we looked at Adam and Eve, we would have immediately noticed their divine souls. Faintly, after a bit of concentration, we would have noticed their bodies as well. Today,

---

[102] During the *Havdalah* ceremony marking the transition from the Sabbath to weekday, there is a custom to hold one's fingernails up toward the candle and look at the reflection of the candlelight in them. This shiny reflection symbolizes the bodies of Adam and Eve before the eating of the fruit. As an aside, Kabbalah teaches the fruit was not an apple, but grapes. Had they waited a short while longer, the grapes would have been squeezed into juice to sanctify an eternal Sabbath of peace. Every Friday night, a *Kiddush* blessing on wine is made to rectify this original action.

[103] Many assume that the only reason for modest dress is to avoid temptation. While this may be the case elsewhere, the Jewish view of modest dress is connected to this idea of clothing demonstrating a royal dignity. Is something of great value left in the open? What is uniquely special is often depreciated when flaunted without regard. In addition, a body that houses a soul inside is covered because in our era—the post-Adam and Eve era—we can mistake the body as the primary aspect of a person.

it's the exact inverse. When looking at another, we immediately see a body. Through much effort and sensitivity, we may notice the faint glimmer of an inner soul.

When we desire something material, we say in the first person: *"I'd love to have that!"* What do our souls—our consciences—usually respond to this temptation? *"You* shouldn't do that; it's a bad idea." Sadly, the soul is in the subconscious backseat and is merely suggesting good ideas. Adam and Eve, as well as certain righteous people after them, lived with their souls as their first-person, primary consciousness.

"Hillel the Elder's students once asked him: 'Master, where are you going?' He replied, 'To bestow kindness upon a guest in the house.' They said to him, 'Every day you have a guest?' He replied, 'Is not my soul a poor guest in the body? Today it is here and tomorrow no longer?'"

Most, if not all, religions have tried to fix this dichotomy of body and soul through "asceticism"—denying the body its pleasures through celibacy, fasting, and an overall detachment from the physical. So, why does Judaism always include great food and fine wine when celebrating a spiritual occasion? Why does it emphasize the spiritual power of marriage, constantly focusing on fusing the material and physical together?

For a reason we can't fully understand, God's primary desire is for this world. His desire is for physical human beings to perform divine acts, and that through these actions we transform the physical world into a conduit for spiritual energy. A mitzvah is a direct connection to the infinite. Through these deeds we also unite body and soul, emulating the matriarch Sarah, whose other name was Yiskah, from the Hebrew word *socheh*—to see through. When people saw Sarah, they saw Godliness. The Torah says that outwardly she was exquisitely beautiful, but it was through her deeds and self-refinement that she was able to become a transparent vessel for the beauty of her soul.

May we soon reach the day when we will be able to see everything and everyone for who they really are inside; their true essence clear for all to see. The mystics teach that in a future time, not only will the body be a transparent vessel that reveals the soul, but the body itself will shine even greater than the soul it houses.

The King's Letter

There once lived a king who had an only son. At a certain point, the king came to the realization that his prince had grown up too sheltered and needed to understand the people of his kingdom if he ever hoped to govern properly. With a heavy heart, the king told his son to pack his bags for a journey. The prince tearfully but obediently left the palace. Dressed like a commoner in order to blend in, he traveled to a distant province of the kingdom and mingled with the people of the city.

As time passed, the prince learned to relate to the common people and empathize with their needs. But he longed for his home and missed his father. One day, a letter arrived from the palace! He excitedly opened it, and found a loving and encouraging letter from his father.

The prince was so overjoyed, he started dancing and singing with great emotion. The village folk looked at him as if he had lost his mind.

"How could they ever hope to understand how I feel right now," thought the prince. "They can't relate to the feeling of receiving such a letter."

The prince walked to the town square, stood on a box, and announced:

"I will be sponsoring a huge party! Everyone to the tavern!"

The villagers excitedly streamed toward the tavern where food and drink were quickly passed around. Everyone began to dance and sing with reckless abandon—no one more so than the prince. But there was one major difference: The commoners were celebrating because of the free food and drink, while the prince was celebrating the loving letter he had received from the king.

***

A major component of the Jewish celebration of holy days is the inclusion of good food and drink: *hallah* bread and wine, fish and meat, fine clothing, and a well-adorned table.[104] "...And you shall call the Sabbath a delight."[105]

On these holy days where a unique light shines, our souls intrinsically sense this light and celebrate wholeheartedly. But since we are made up of souls placed in bodies that only understand material matters, how can the interests of our soul possibly excite our material-minded psyches into celebration? This is why we make the experience enjoyable for the body as well.

Like the prince who gives the commoners material pleasures they can relate to, we, too celebrate with the best the world has to offer on the Sabbath and the holidays. All our faculties must enjoy this day. We sing and dance in joyful celebration of this special time as we feel closeness with our King whom we haven't seen in a while. But as our bodies celebrate with delicious food and drink,[106] our souls celebrate the spiritual energy present in the air.

Elul—As Accessible as Air

"In our village, when the month of Elul came, one could feel it in the air."[107]

***

---

[104] Not necessarily meat or fish, but whatever one finds pleasure in is the main thing (Mishna Berurah 242:1).

[105] Isaiah 58:13.

[106] However, unlike the commoners who are given food and drink that have no value other than physical pleasure, Kabbalah teaches that the physical pleasures on the Sabbath and holidays actually become spiritual in nature. The holiness of the time uplifts the materiality of the actions and items into their source above. The analogy of the commoners applies in that our primary focus on these days is still the elevation of the soul.

[107] Rabbi Joseph Isaac Schneersohn, *Likkutei Dibburim*, Part 1, p. 230.

In the late-eighteenth century, there lived a notable hassid by the name of Shmuel Munkis, an ardent follower of the renowned Rabbi Shneur Zalman of Liadi. Whenever the high holidays drew near, Shmuel would prepare to travel the great distance to his beloved teacher for the inspiration he needed to approach these special days properly. However, this year there was a little problem. Shmuel had no money. Any poor villager who wanted to travel knew he had but one option: travel by foot, even in the freezing Russian winter.

Undeterred, Shmuel set off for the town of his rabbi. As he trudged along the side of the road under torrents of snow, a wagon pulled up beside him. The driver called out to Shmuel and asked him his destination. Seeing as they were heading in the same direction, he told Shmuel to hop on. Lucky as he was to find a ride, he was still forced to sit in the back of the wagon under the open sky, surrounded by the driver's barrels of liquor. Freezing, he turned to the driver and asked if it would be okay if he took a small drink from one of the barrels. As he sipped from his cup, Shmuel began to finally feel some warmth enter his body.

After reaching his destination, Shmuel ran straight into the synagogue and called his friends over to sit with him.

He explained: "I learned something on my way here. I realized that a person can be surrounded by potential warmth. But if he doesn't internalize that warmth, he will remain cold."

***

To fully appreciate a special moment, we have to *drink it in*, not just experience it. We can be surrounded by wonderful practices and prayers, witness a moving scene, stand in an ancient place, or hear inspiring words of wisdom. But if we don't identify with and integrate it, failing to strongly connect with the message of that moment, then we can't internalize its warmth.

The most essential things in life are often the most accessible, like the air we breathe. It sustains life and is everywhere. A bit less essential and therefore less accessible, is food and water. But, even though something is vital to our lives, because it is so accessible, we take it for granted. Nothing is more vital and accessible to us than our own heartbeat, yet how often do we think about it?

In relationships as well, we often take for granted those who are most important to us, such as our family or spouse. As essential as they are in our lives, because they're always around, we forget to appreciate how valuable they are. We see this in our spiritual lives as well. According to Jewish law, next to Yom Kippur, it's surprising to discover that Shabbat is considered the holiest day of the year.[108] Because we have it every week, however, we can forget its unique spiritual power.

Air may be plentiful, but to enjoy the benefits of the oxygen that's all around us, we have to actually breathe it in. Without this simple action, life doesn't begin. So too, no matter how much we are blessed with, if we lack an awareness of those blessings, we will miss out on the joy that gratitude for these blessing brings. We are given special opportunities for inspiration and wisdom, especially in the months of Elul and Tishrei. God is always close by, but the usual obstacles that challenge our feelings of connection are temporarily lifted at this time. Everything is clearer. The additional prayers and other traditions of these two months provide more opportunities to connect with the Divine. But we often ignore these opportunities for connection, and even if we find a moment of inspiration, it can leave as fast as it came. What's needed is a will to internalize and actualize this inspiration for the long run.

Developing our spiritual awareness takes constant internalization. *Emunah* (faith) stems from the word *amon* (craftsman). Like a craftsman who continually labors day and night, it takes consistent effort to internalize our beliefs. At this time of year we hone our craft, but this shouldn't stop once

---

[108] According to Jewish law, the Sabbath is treated as the holiest of days. Spiritually speaking, the Talmud says: "If Israel were to keep two Sabbaths, they would be redeemed immediately" (Shabbat 118b).

the holidays are over. Moments of inspiration are fleeting and infatuation never lasts. Relationships are nurtured through consistent effort and care. Through this effort we will start to feel how the connection our soul has with God is as accessible as the air we breathe and as sweet and invigorating as a warm drink on a cold winter's night.

Yom Kippur—Inside the Palace Gates

The holiest day of the Jewish year is Yom Kippur—The Day of Atonement—a rare, twenty-four-hour space in time with a powerful spiritual energy conducive to returning to our inherent good nature.[109] If a person is far removed from his spiritual self, enmeshed in mundane desires for 364 days, how can it be possible to turn toward good in an instant? The *Baal Shem Tov* offered a parable to illustrate this.

***

Once there was a king who decided his son had finally grown old enough to go off into the world to learn his own life lessons and acquire wisdom. He wished him well, gave him plenty of money and provisions for the journey, and sent him off in a royal carriage. Days later, the prince passed a town that attracted him. He told his driver to halt and decided to settle there.

As often happens in life, the prince became accustomed to the manner of his environment and exchanged his royal ways for the local customs, drinking at the taverns and partying the nights away. His royal upbringing in the palace with the king all faded into the background. Years passed, until one day he realized that his vast wealth had been exhausted. Soon he looked like the poorest of villagers, dusty and tired. After working a few dead-end jobs, the once regal prince was now wearing tattered clothing and had barely a penny to his name. One night, as he walked the empty streets, a memory of his old life popped into his head.

---

[109] This renewal of connection with the divine is called *Teshuva*. Often improperly translated as "repentance," its true translation is "return." This slight variation is significant, as it signifies that even when we err, our natural state remains pure and wholesome, and we can return at any time.

70

"I'm a prince! What am I still doing here? I miss my father and the palace!"

The prince left on foot, and after a three-week journey, he finally entered his city and strode joyfully to the palace gates, ready for a royal reception.

"What do you want!?" barked the palace guards at the tattered wayfarer in front of them. Startled, it dawned on the prince that not only had he lost his royal appearance, he had even forgotten how to speak his native language properly. As he was being roughly pushed away from the gates, the helpless prince let out a piercing cry of longing from the depths of his heart. The king, standing by a palace window, immediately felt his heart melt. It was his son! He had been waiting so long for his return. He ran outside and tearfully embraced his prince.

***

In life, we mess up and sometimes lose our way. But what we *do* does not define who we *are* at the core of our being. The mystics teach that one's soul may be covered over by negativity but can never be tainted. A diamond covered in dirt is still a diamond. The soul is waiting to be awakened in a moment of longing for its divine source. On Yom Kippur we pray five times, with each prayer corresponding to one of the five levels of the soul. The final prayer before the day ends is known as *ne'ilah*—the closing of the gates, which corresponds to *yechidah*—the fifth level: the essence of the soul.

The simple understanding of this prayer is that the gates of heaven are closing as Yom Kippur comes to an end, and this is the last chance to beseech God for a good year. At this time the gates are closing, but with us on the inside. Here, one is completely unified alone with God, who wants only the best for us.

We may have strayed far from the palace, but we can return at any moment. God accepts us even after we've sinned, allowing us to fix past mistakes. The mystics teach that this is only possible because our souls are rooted in a higher place in God than His commandments. But in order to fix mistakes, we must first acknowledge them and make a firm decision to change. The prophet Isaiah says: "Shake off the dust and arise."[110] If your rooster is covered in dust, you can try to painstakingly pull every piece out of its feathers. But if the rooster decides on its own to shake with all its might, the dust is removed in an instant. Real change can only be produced from a desire within.

On this day, we can tap into our true selves. The pure cries of the ram's horn and of our prayers are like the simple cries of the prince for the king, our soul's yearning for her divine king. We may have forgotten the language of connection during the last year, but the moment we cry out, our father will receive us with love, ensuring his princes and princesses a good and sweet year.

Sukkot—The Humble Hut of Trust

A Frenchman immigrated to Tel Aviv, Israel in 1990. In 1991, Iraq fired thirty-nine scud missiles on Israel, the majority at Tel Aviv. To imagine the destructive force of even one scud missile, that same year Iraq hit a US base in Saudi Arabia with one, killing twenty-seven and wounding ninety-eight. Yet in Israel on that night, the missiles exacted zero casualties. He remarked that his life changed after recognizing God's watchful protection at that time.[111]

As the Jewish nation escaped Ancient Egypt, they wandered for forty years through the desert on their way to Israel. The Torah tells us that throughout the journey, God sheltered the people from danger with "clouds of glory." As a remembrance of this protection, each year for seven days[112] Jews leave their comfortable homes for a humble hut called a *sukkah*.

---

[110] Isaiah 52:2.

[111] As much violence as there is in the Middle East, we are taught that Israel will always be as safe a place as any to live in: "The eyes of God are upon the Land of Israel from the beginning of the year to the end of the year" (Deuteronomy 11:12).

[112] Outside of Israel, the holiday is celebrated for eight days.

"Live in sukkot for seven days, so that your generations will know that I [the Lord] had the Israelites live in booths when I brought them out of Egypt."[113] For these seven days, all eating, drinking, and even leisure activity are to occur inside the *sukkah*, which serves as a temporary home.

The flimsy outdoor dwelling of the *sukkah* represents our dependence on and trust in a greater power beyond ourselves. Throughout the year, we live under a sturdy shelter that meets all of our comforts. But as we sit inside the humble *sukkah* walls, feeling the open breeze of the night sky, we are reminded of a higher force beyond the secure walls of our home, the source of good we experience all year long when under a roof. The *sukkah* reminds us that all of our blessings come from above.

As King David concludes with the last verse in the Book of Psalms: "My entire soul will bless God, may God be blessed."[114] The Hebrew term for "soul" is spelled the same as the word for "breath."[115] King David is teaching us that we should acknowledge every blessing, even the simple taking of a momentary breath.

On a deeper level, King David is also addressing a fundamental question: "Where is God?" *He is everywhere at all times,* says David. But just as we fail to take notice of our breathing, even though it is constant and our bodies are surrounded by air, we do the same with God. We are submerged in His divine energy and yet we fail to notice it. On Sukkot, we work on internalizing an awareness that there is nothing to be fearful of, since God is everywhere, watching over us at every moment.

***

There was a businessman living in New York City who found himself in dire financial straits. With no other choice, he called his very wealthy best friend and explained his situation.

---

[113] Leviticus 23:42-43.

[114] Psalms 150:6.

[115] *Neshamah* (soul) and *Neshima* (breath).

"I'm happy to help you with whatever you need," his friend reassured him. That afternoon, he headed to his friend's penthouse on the thirty-ninth floor of his forty-floor building. After gratefully receiving the funds he needed, he realized he was only one flight below the rooftop and decided to take in the beautiful view of the Manhattan skyline at sunset.

Seeing the view, he began to relax for the first time in a while. Suddenly, his thoughts were interrupted by the sound of the rooftop door slamming shut. Walking over with a feeling of dread, he found the door locked. He banged on the door, but no response came. He ran over to the edge of the roof and shouted toward the street below, but no one could hear him. With no other option, the man reluctantly began pulling out a few of his new 20-dollar notes and dropping them over the edge to alert passersby. Looking on in disbelief, he saw the people on the street grabbing the bills floating in the wind, paying no attention to his plight forty floors above. At wit's end, the man scanned his surroundings and spotted a pile of pebbles. Scooping them together, he proceeded to drop them below, hitting a few pedestrians on their heads. The damaged parties looked straight up to the roof and shouted angrily. Soon the police arrived to arrest the stranded man, who then explained what had happened, and was finally released to go on his way.

***

When life is going just as planned, we tend to take our health, wealth, and comfort for granted. Rarely do we look up and thank the one above for the gifts we receive. It's only when things are painful that we look up to complain. The painful things also have a reason, and are for a purpose, coming from the same benevolent source. The same one who sends us dollar bills from the sky is also the one hitting us with pebbles.

It takes great mindfulness and sensitivity to recognize our blessings. Sadly, it's a staple of the human condition to truly appreciate something only when it's missing. Only when we're sick do we appreciate our health. When bad events occur, we may not understand the hidden reason behind them. But neither can an ant fathom the intentions of a human being. To know God is to be God; anything we actually do understand is only a divine kindness. What seems from our limited vantage point as negative could be the greatest blessing. If an alien visiting earth were shown an operating room, they would scream for all to stop the cruel surgeon from hurting the patient. But the surgeon is actually *saving* the patient. As the mystics teach: "No evil descends from above."[116] Let's work on our awareness of all the good in our lives, while remembering that our challenges are for a purpose, coming from the same benevolent source.

Hanukkah—Doughnuts, Latkes, and Oil

The winter holiday of Hanukkah is known as the "Festival of Lights" for the *menorah* candelabra we light for eight nights. This lighting recalls the great miracle of the small jar of oil that had enough light for one night, but stayed lit for eight nights in the Temple of Jerusalem. There is a custom on the holiday to eat oily foods, such as *sufganiyot* doughnuts and potato pancake *latkes*. While the menorah lighting has inspiring symbolism, why are the doughnuts necessary? They, too commemorate the discovery of one last jar of pure olive oil, but what's the deeper meaning of this custom?[117]

Before the miracle of lights, another miracle occurred when the tiny army of Maccabees defeated the great Syrian Greek army. The Greeks had been trying to eradicate Jewish traditions. While in the times of Purim,[118] a decree was passed to allow for the murder of the Jewish people, on

---

[116] Tanya, Iggeret Hakodesh, Epistle 11. The things that happen to us that appear as bad, come from a deeper spiritual place than the good.

[117] Another custom on Hanukkah is to play with a *dreidel* (spinning top), which was originally used by Jewish children as a diversion when Greek soldiers approached them. This was to avoid being caught learning Torah, a forbidden and punishable offense. On a deeper level, the dreidel—which is spun from its top, causing it to rotate at its bottom—signifies how a divine power was controlling the miraculous events of Hanukkah, *spinning* the world below. Incidentally, there is a custom on the holiday of *Purim* to rotate a *gragger* (noisemaker) during the reading of the *Megillah* (story of Esther). This rotation of the lower handle that spins the upper portion symbolizes how the Jewish nation affected God's Will for their salvation at that time, from below to above.

[118] Discussed in next chapter.

Hanukkah, the persecution wasn't on the Jewish *body*, but on their belief system. It was, in essence, a war on the spirit.

The ancient Greeks valued the aesthetic beauty of the human body and pursuit of intellectual endeavors in the arts, music and philosophy, including such greats as Socrates, Plato, Homer, and Aristotle.

In light of where Greek ancestry is rooted in the Torah, this emphasis on external beauty makes perfect sense. In the Book of Genesis, after the great flood, Noah blesses Shem—from whom Abraham descends, hence the term *Semites*—with spiritual truth. He then blesses his son Yefet—from whom *Yavan*, the ancestor of the Greek Empire, descends—with beauty. Noah's wish is that this beauty of Yefet—and later Greece—"should be found in the tents of Shem."[119] Noah saw that true beauty is found when in a meaningful spiritual context.

If the Greek culture coveted beauty and intellectual profundity, then what irked them about the Torah?

Many who don't believe in the divine origin of the Torah, still derive great joy from the wisdom and insight found in the Talmud and the Torah's ethical teachings. In 2011, the South Korean ambassador to Israel remarked: "Each Korean family has at least one copy of the Talmud."[120]

The Greek value placed on intellect and the exploration into the meaning of life could have fused wonderfully with Torah, fulfilling Noah's vision of spiritual beauty and aesthetic beauty coming together in harmony. There was even a point in history when this occurred. The Talmud discusses how the legendary Alexander the Great, upon greeting the leading Jewish Sage of his time, Shimon Hatzadik, "alighted from his chariot and bowed down before him."[121] Indeed, a meaningful relationship

---

[119] Genesis 9:27.

[120] From an article on the website of the *New Yorker*, written by Ross Arbes.

[121] Yoma 69a.

and exchange of ideas between Greek—and later Roman—rulers and the Sages occurred on a regular basis with great mutual respect.[122]

The problem wasn't that the Greeks were bothered by the intellectual beauty found in Torah. They enjoyed it. What bothered them were those who treated its wisdom as anything more than just a set of ideas. The Jewish people weren't treating Torah and its mitzvot as interesting customs and tradition, but as a divine will that just happened to be expressed through intellect. That's a big difference. The Jewish view is that there exists a reality beyond what a human mind can ever reach on its own. This is not an illogical belief that disregards logic, but a belief in what *transcends* limited human logic. This the Greeks could not tolerate.

Jewish mysticism and Hassidut most reveal the transcendent nature of Torah wisdom that the Greeks despised. The mystics liken this deep wisdom to oil.[123] Oil poured into any substance will pervade it thoroughly. The inner dimension of Torah, too pervades all of reality; every aspect of creation hints to its wisdom.[124]

Oil is difficult to consume raw.[125] To properly absorb oil, we cook, combine, or fry it together with something more edible. The necessity of mixing raw oil with dough or potatoes and onions in order to be properly digested, symbolizes the need for divine wisdom to be expressed in an intellectually tangible, *edible* way.[126]

---

[122] Avodah Zarah 10. Nedarim 50b, et al.

[123] See: Schneerson, Menachem M. On the Essence of Chassidus, p. 46-48. New York: Kehot, 1998.

[124] Yalkut Shimoni, Mishlei 942: "God looked into the Torah and created the world."

[125] There's a discussion in the Talmud as to whether there should be a special blessing for oil. Just as wine has a distinct blessing from its grape source, shouldn't oil have a special blessing from olives, like *borei pri hazayit?* The Talmud concludes against this, since oil *on its own* is damaging. Try downing a full cup of olive oil every morning!

[126] The process of eating is similar to the process of understanding an idea. An abstract idea needs to be broken down into bite-sized smaller details to be understood properly. Just as digested food becomes part of your body, an idea—when properly internalized in your mind—changes you.

On its own, *raw* Divinity would be too overwhelming for us to absorb. But by *cooking* and *baking* this supernal wisdom into tangible words and ideas that our minds can consume, we are able to internalize the lofty wisdom contained within them. This is why Torah is made up of practical laws, stories and lessons we can grasp. While seemingly simple, they contain the deepest wisdom within.

Every human relationship, aspect of nature, scientific and psychological observation contains insight into God's thoughts. But if we had the ability to see the divine wisdom behind all things—spiritual worlds, angels, and the greatest of secrets—our limited minds could not handle it. God, therefore, condensed His wisdom—His oil—into *donuts* and *latkes* we could internalize; so condensed, in fact, that the words on paper could appear to the Greeks as just another set of wise teachings and nothing more. The custom to eat these oily foods on Hanukkah thus symbolizes the process God uses to feed our minds with deep wisdom that we can digest.

How can we be expected to draw inspiration from hidden wisdom we can't see? Whether or not we sense anything when we learn Torah, the divine essence inside—like oil—seeps into our inner being and awakens our soul's inner essence. But instead of physical heartburn, this type of oil inspires a spiritual heartburn—a fire of the heart—since *the soul, Torah, and God are all essentially one.*[127]

Through learning and refining ourselves, the aesthetic beauty of Greece can fulfill its purpose in the tents of Shem, a beauty that reflects depth and meaning. As we delve into the Torah's wisdom, we must remember that these teachings aren't intellect, but Godliness condensed into ideas. The inner essence of the words will then begin to uncover the inner connection we have with its giver.

---

[127] Zohar 3:73a.

Purim—Behind the Mask

The fourteenth day of the Hebrew month of Adar commemorates the holiday of Purim. This day marks the events in ancient Persia 2,400 years ago when Haman and his plan to exterminate the Jewish people were defeated.[128] Haman had made a *raffle* (*pur* in Hebrew, hence the name of the holiday) to help him decide on a date for the annihilation of the Jews. After receiving the approval of the king, Haman sent an edict throughout the lands, giving permission for all to attack any Jew on the fourteenth day of Adar with impunity. Unfortunately for Haman, Queen Esther happened to be a hidden Jew, and together with her uncle Mordecai, she convinced the king to denounce the wicked Haman, and the Jewish people were saved.

These events were recorded by Esther—one of the seven prophetesses in the *Tanakh*[129]—and entitled *Megillat Esther.* This Scroll of Esther is read every year on Purim, and the day is celebrated as one of the happiest of the year with costumes and parties. Special cookies with a sweet filling are eaten—called *hamantaschen*— named after the three-cornered hat that Haman wore. Purim is an intriguing story of persecution and salvation, with a king, queen, hero, and villain. But what personal relevance does it have to our lives today, thousands of years later?

Out of the twenty-four books of the Tanakh, the Scroll of Esther is the only book that makes zero mention of God.[130] One could argue, this is because the events of Purim seem to have unfolded in a natural manner. The Jewish people do prevail under dire circumstances, but with Esther as queen and the influential Mordecai also in a position of power, perhaps

---

[128] This story was recently depicted (somewhat accurately) in the major motion picture film of 2006, *One Night with the King.*

[129] Hebrew acronym for the Five Books of Moses, Prophets and Writings.

[130] King Solomon's "Song of Songs" makes no clear mention of God, either. However, there are clear references, such as the name Hamakom, 'the place," which our Sages say is a reference to God who exists in every place.

it was simply a case of being in the right place at the right time. Was there anything miraculous about it?

The theme of Purim focuses precisely on this idea.

Although God's name is conspicuously absent from the Megillah, He's very much present, directing the improbable sequence of events behind the scenes. Like the Purim story, the events of our personal lives also seem to unfold naturally without any outside influence. But every detail is actually being guided behind the scenes.

The word *megillah* is connected to the word *megaleh*—to reveal. The Talmud states that Esther's name is connected to the word *hester*—being hidden. Thus, *Megillat Esther* means *revealing what is hidden.* The story of Purim symbolizes the challenge of revealing the hidden divine influence in our lives.

We can now better understand the customs associated with this holiday. Costumes and masks conceal the identity of their wearer. Our world serves as a mask that hides God's presence. The challenge is to recognize that the world we see is merely a well-fitted costume, each detail chosen to express a specific aspect of the one hiding behind it. Once we do, the one who hides has no more reason to hide His identity.[131] The mask begins to come off, and a more intimate relationship with the one behind the disguise can then begin.

Events that seem difficult to understand have a sweet reason behind them. When Haman erected gallows to hang Mordecai, who would have thought that this would lead to a positive outcome? Yet on the appointed day for destruction, it was Haman who was instead hung on those very

---

[131] This explains why certain righteous people are able to perform miracles, bending the laws of nature. This person has reached a level of divine awareness where he recognizes that nature is simply a mask for a higher divine power. He has called out God's name behind the mask of nature. God then has no need to hide from that person anymore. The bending of the rules of nature for him will not alter his freedom of choice, but will only reveal what he already knows to be true. See Talmud, Taanit 24b-25a for examples of this. To explore in greater depth, see the book *Worldmask,* p. 27, 37 and throughout.

gallows, and a day of defeat was turned into a momentous victory. This is why on Purim we eat hamantaschen cookies whose inner sweetness is hidden inside a hardened cookie.

Why is the holiday named after Haman's lottery to decide the date of the Jewish destruction? Wouldn't this be the least desirable reference for a holiday? Haman wanted to show the world that all of life is a lottery. Things happen by chance, without reason. The salvation of the Jewish people against all odds showed that life is the very opposite. God hides in order to give us free choice to either recognize His role or not, avoiding supernatural miracles whenever possible. But even when the sea doesn't split and God's voice isn't heard thundering from the heavens, we are shown glimpses behind the mask of reality that we can recognize as His hand at work.

Our lives are one long Megillah Scroll, where daily events are guided by a hidden hand of providence, each personal story planned to lead to a good and purposeful destination.[132] What seems to be abandonment in our darkest times will instead lead to "light and happiness, joy and glory."[133]

Passover—Harmonious Balance

Today, it's hard to ignore the emphasis placed on being in shape, exercising regularly, eating right, and doing everything we can to live a long and healthy life. But it's been documented in the medical world that healthy living isn't only related to one's waistline or muscle workout but also to one's mind and inner well-being.

---

[132] In continuation of this theme, notice Esther's actions when confronted with the possible decimation of her people. Esther is charged with pleading to the king to find mercy. Surely the first thing Esther would do is put on makeup and beautify herself in order to gain favor before the king. Instead, she prays and fasts for three days! (This is commemorated today by fasting on the day before Purim.) Esther recognized that everything was in the hands of God, not the king. She had to do her part within nature to plead to the king for mercy, with the knowledge that ultimately the fate of her people and the final decision would be decided by the King of kings.

[133] Scroll of Esther 8:16.

The greatest of Sages, with Maimonides (1135-1204) at the forefront, taught that the path to good health comes through living a *balanced* life. Since "Man is a miniature world,"[134] the human need for balance and harmony must pervade all of reality. Balance is an essential element of our world: Too much sugar can cause diabetes while low blood sugar can lead to hypoglycemia. Too many bacteria-fighting white blood cells is *neutrophilia*, while too few is *neutropenia*, both leading to ill health. Our lungs breathe in and then out. Our heart contracts inward and pumps outward. The waves of the ocean dash forward to shore only to return back to the sea. An imbalance in any of these areas can lead to catastrophic results.

Just as we need physical balance for optimal functionality, we also need mental and emotional balance. We strive and accomplish with all of our might, but this ambition must be balanced with time for relaxation and restoration, quality moments with loved ones and for sleep. Raising children also requires a balance of unconditional love with expectations and boundaries.

Modern society, with its technological advancements and fast-paced culture focused on business achievement, often makes living a balanced life challenging. What was once an intimate family dinner is now a cell phone dinner. A home filled with family values is now filled with superficial pop culture. Children are told how to dress, look, act, and think cool, regardless of what it takes. With the challenges of our generation, we can still excel by creating boundaries and order, deciding what enters our bodies, minds, homes, and families, in a balanced way.

Internal emotional balance and structure are equally essential to a healthy life. We can feel warmth and a love forothers while having the sensitivity and respect to give room when needed. In the heavenly realms, we see this concept in the vision of Ezekiel, where he describes the

---

[134] Maimonides, Guide to the Perplexed, 1:72.

angels as "running and returning,"[135] reaching in love toward God but then withdrawing in awe, keeping a healthy distance and boundary. One of the core principles in Jewish mysticism is that every spiritual realm is characterized by divine emanations called *sefirot*. The sefira identified with the attribute of truth is *tiferet*—harmony.[136] Our ability to harmonize kindness and giving with discipline and restraint is the path of truth.

Every holiday has a unique spiritual energy connected to the original events it commemorates that resurfaces every year on that date. The specific energy that infuses Passover is *freedom*; more specifically, a *structure that leads to freedom*. On the first night of Passover, it is an ancient Jewish tradition to speak in detail about the journey of freedom from Egypt and the miracles that led to it, known as a *pesach seder*. *Pesach* means "leaping,"[137] while *seder* means "order." What a total contradiction! The seder, however, is a program of "ordered leaping," spiritually rooted customs set in an order that enables us to leap to spiritual heights—a balanced order that leads to transcendence.

This is how music works. A song inspires and uplifts us to the greatest of heights, succeeding because of its structure, harmony and rhythm of sound.[138] Like music, a healthy structure allows us to transcend that structure, maximizing our talents and abilities in the process. This motif

---

[135] Ezekiel 1:14. This concept is known as *ratzo va'shov* and is found on every spiritual level, as souls and angels reach upward to receive new energy and inspiration from the Divine. God, too does the same, known in the Mystical works as mati v'lo mati, giving forth new divine energy to enliven creation, then drawing it back.

[136] This *sefira* is also defined as "compassion" and "beauty." The kabbalists explain that beauty is achieved through the blending of various colors as opposed to only one. So, too the ability to harmonize various emotions like kindness and severity, love and awe, is truly beautiful.

[137] Exodus 11:13. This commemorates God's leaping/passing over of the homes of the Jewish people during the death plague of the Egyptian male first-born.

[138] This structure in music that is also found in the rest of reality is connected to the number seven. There are seven notes in the Western music scale (C-D-E-F-G-A-B) and seven colors in a rainbow (red, yellow, green, blue, violet, orange and indigo). The Torah describes seven days of formation that make up our week. Each of the seven has a unique energy connected to the corresponding divine *sefira* of that day: Kindness/Love, Strength/Restraint, Compassion/Harmony, Endurance/Victory, Humility/Splendor, Bonding/Foundation, Action/Kingship.

is seen throughout our lives. When starting a passion project or working on a fitness goal, intense hours of disciplined work are exerted over long periods of time to reach a goal. Far from feeling enslaved, a deep feeling of joy and freedom permeates the work of those people because the effort is an actualization of their inner purpose.

Judaism is full of rules and order. There are specific times to pray and fulfill commandments. But far from trying to constrict and box us in, they are ordered methods meant to help us connect to the Infinite and get in touch with our deepest selves, leaping to places that transcend our usual human abilities. A child might enjoy dialing seventy numbers into a cell phone at random, but there are specific combinations that will result in a connection with a being on the other line who chose those numbers for a reason.[139] This harmony of spiritual intention fused with physical actions is at the core of Judaism.

But doesn't *freedom* mean that we have the ability to do whatever we want, whenever we want to? That approach may actually be a form of selfish individualism as slaves to our every desire. An addict is free to begin his addiction through following his desire.[140] On the Sabbath when we're told to stop taking work calls, turn off our social media, and live in the moment, is that freedom or slavery to rules? Real freedom comes when we

---

[139] Even when engaged in lofty activities like prayer or meditation, our goal is always to take that inspiration we experience and bring it down into our day-to-day lives, to better the world practically. This harmony of spiritual intention fused with physical actions is at the core of Judaism. In the Talmud, we learn of a fascinating event where the greatest sages ascended to paradise through meditation. Only one, Rabbi Akiva, "entered in peace, and left in peace." By *entering* the loftiest of experiences with the intention of later *leaving* to return to earthly reality, he was able to properly succeed (Hagigah 14b).

[140] In the late 1990s, a well-known *gangster-rapper* by the name of Shyne—a protégé of Sean "P. Diddy" Combs—was arrested and sentenced to ten years in prison for his role in a nightclub shooting. During the Purim holiday of 2008, I visited a prison in upstate New York together with friends to bring joy to the Jewish inmates for the holiday. There we met Shyne who had converted to Judaism during his incarceration years earlier. In an interview after his release in 2009, Shyne explained how the structure he found in Judaism with boundaries of right and wrong and the importance of living a balanced life gave an order to his world of chaos; his childhood had been "free" — wild and without boundaries, but he had felt imprisoned by it.

are able to express our true selves at the core of who we are. On Passover we are given a greater chance at realizing a state of freedom that not only isn't ruled by a physical force, but is a liberation of the soul from our negative tendencies.[141] This comes through mastering our internal drives, tempering emotional instincts with what our mind and soul knows is best for us.

Maimonides teaches: "The upright path is the middle path." However, there are two exceptions that Maimonides lists, that must be avoided to the extreme: *anger* and *ego*.[142] Sometimes, we need to utilize extreme methods in certain areas in order to reach balance.[143] On Passover, we don't just lessen or balance our hametz intake; it's eradicated completely! This is because *humility* is symbolized by the *matzah* cracker that is flat, while the forbidden bread, called *hametz*, is bloated and puffed up, symbolizing *ego* and self-centeredness.[144]

Strangely, matzah and hametz aren't very different from each another. Matzah and hametz are officially separated by only a few extra minutes, even seconds, of baking flour in an oven! But that's the point: Matzah is simply *disciplined* bread, an ordered existence with boundaries that symbolizes the crucial importance of having a healthy structure that enables us to live lives of balance and freedom, leaping to progressively greater heights.

---

[141] Passover has an energy that we can tap into to reach inner freedom. Once we locate an area in our lives that's in need of balancing, we can choose to ride the spiritual energy of the moment to break free of its shackles. Mistakes are normal. We aren't expected to eliminate our animalistic desires, but rather to work on taming and channeling them in a positive direction.

[142] Laws of Understanding, 1:4.

[143] Maimonides teaches that any trait we have a big problem with can be fixed through acting in the other extreme for a short time. One who is stingy should practice giving a large sum of charity once or twice. Someone who never listens to others should practice listening in total silence, which will help to later reach a balanced place.

[144] The Hebrew word *matzah* has the same letters as *hametz*, except for having a ה instead of a ח. The ה of matzah with its opening at the top of the letter symbolizes one with a humble, open spirit who has made room for a connection from below to above. The ח of hametz is closed above, symbolizing one who is full of oneself, which causes there to be no room for God in his life. As Rav Hisda in Sotah 5a, remarked: "Every Man in whom is haughtiness of spirit, God declares, I and he cannot both dwell in the world."

Why Egypt?

Passover is a holiday full of asking questions. During the seder, questions, answers and debates are discussed in the *Haggadah* as a way of remembering the miracles during the exodus from Egypt. But one fundamental question is absent: Why was it necessary for God to allow the Jewish nation to endure so many years of slavery in Egypt in the first place? Surely, Jacob and his sons could have remained happily settled in the land of Israel where their descendants could later receive the Torah instead of Mount Sinai in the Egyptian desert? What was the divine intention here?

Every nation that's abused the Jewish people has had one thing in common: Whether it's Egypt and Babylonia, Greece and Rome, or Spain and later Germany, all were not only uniquely powerful nations; they also led the world in cultural advancement during their time.

In ancient Greece and Rome, the world witnessed amazing achievements in democracy, philosophy, and intellectual debate. Spain saw a golden age of art, literature, and world exploration, while Germany greatly valued the arts, architecture, movies, and music. These nations were at the forefront of their time—*enlightened.*

High culture and sophistication, however, does not equate to a morally upright society. Culture isn't Torah. Artistic, technological, and athletic achievements may induce great joy and wonder, but are not necessarily recipes for goodness. As impressive as these skills are, they do not address the topic of morality and character. In Nazi Germany, the kind treatment of animals, especially dogs, is well known. On an individual level, from Mozart to Beethoven to many intellectual giants and popular figures that shaped the culture of their time, living a morally upright personal life was far from a priority. Torah was given to the world in order to change the inner self, to refine the animal within, making one into a *mensch.*[145] The youth in our school system would greatly benefit from an inclusion of

---

[145] A Yiddish term used to refer to an ethical human being.

values and ethical discussions, emphasizing the importance of moral action beyond only academic success.

We can now answer that fundamental question of why the Israelites had to live in Egypt as a precursor to accepting the Torah. Without living in Egypt, the people may have always wondered: *Look at the pyramids, mathematics, and hieroglyphics! Aren't we missing out on learning from Egypt, the most advanced culture in the world? Can this Torah ideology really aid our lives any better than the wisdom of this cutting-edge nation?*

God therefore decided: *I will first send them to experience the outcomes of this advanced culture.*

For all of its advancement, Egyptian society was morally deficient.[146] Despite their great contributions, the nations of the world never offered the ethical monotheism of the Torah.[147] When the Hebrews finally left Egypt, they were able to truly appreciate what they later received at Mount Sinai.

The Torah and its guiding principles are a vital resource for living a just and moral life. Much of the societal progress we take for granted today, such as the value of human life, justice, education, and social responsibility, stem from the Torah.[148] Some argue that at this progressive point in history we inherently know what to do and what not to do, without advice from any ancient teachings. Why turn to religion that has produced most of the violence and evil in our world? But we have seen in the twentieth century, where approximately one to two hundred million deaths resulted from leaders who were completely devoid of religious belief,[149] that evil can

---

[146] For one example of the cruelty of that era (New Kingdom), see: Gretchen R. Dabbs, Melissa Zabecki. Slot-type fractures of the scapula at New Kingdom Tell El-Amarna, Egypt. IJPP, Elsevier. Netherlands: 2015.

[147] The United States, however, is the first leading nation in history to fully embrace ideas of Torah. Many of its ideals can be found in the US Constitution and its societal makeup. On the Liberty Bell is written: "Proclaim Liberty throughout all the land" (Leviticus 25:10). For more, see the writings of Dennis Prager on the subject.

[148] See *Worldperfect: The Jewish Impact on Civilization*, Ken Spiro, for the far-reaching effects the Torah has had on the moral progression of humanity.

[149] Jozef Stalin in Russia, Adolf Hitler in Germany, and Mao Zedong in China.

come from any place. We have seen that in a completely secular society, a culture of moral relativism is a real possibility. By now, we should be wary of systems of thought devoid of any Torah values.

By looking to the Torah for guidance, we place a cosmic emphasis on the human responsibility to improve our world.

Shavuot: Mass Revelation

The holiday of *Shavuot* commemorates the moment God gave the Torah to the Jewish people on Mount Sinai in Egypt. Many belief systems claim to have been divinely inspired. What's unique about this event that formed the basis for Judaism?

A religion generally begins with one person who professes to have had a direct revelation from a Supreme Being. This individual alone experienced the word of God and wants to share the newfound teachings with others. These devoted adherents then preach their new religion to followers who believe in their validity. But how can we verify if the original teachings were divinely inspired?

We find one striking exception to this narrative. The foundation of Judaism is based on a bold claim: Approximately three million men, women, and children—its entire nation at the time—witnessed firsthand a revelation of God who spoke directly with them and taught the Ten Commandments. This revelation was accepted not only by the Jewish people of the time, but also by later belief systems, including Christianity. Later belief systems may have claimed to be a new path from God, but they never tried to refute the Jewish claim.

A mass revelation is certainly more powerful than an individual one, so why was this claim never duplicated? The answer is simple. When someone claims a private spiritual experience, it's impossible to refute it. But to convince an entire nation that they *themselves* witnessed a mass revelation is a risky endeavor. If even one comes forward to deny witnessing this revelation and its principles, the foundation will crumble. Judaism made this claim, yet we find no dissent from its people anywhere in Jewish history, even under the threat of torture and death.

Beginning with the national experience at Sinai and continuing throughout history, not only was the entire nation of Jews meticulous in their observance of the 613 commandments of the Torah; they consistently gave up their lives in loyalty to that revelation at Sinai. From a people obsessed with the value of life, this self-sacrifice—and observance of any of the difficult commandments for that matter—came from a tradition of Divine revelation that was passed down with such intense passion from parent to child that no other option was imaginable to them, even under the threat of death.

One may argue that this was over three thousand years ago; the revelation at Sinai is too far back in history to verify regardless of whether one or a million people accepted the claim. The same people can, however, believe without a doubt that the Declaration of Independence was written by the founding fathers. They never saw it happen or have any pictures of the event, but the proof is that it's only a few hundred years old, and we have the original documents today as well as the words of witnesses from the time.

Let's try and apply this logic to the revelation at Sinai: If adults who witnessed this original revelation gave this experience over as an oral tradition to their children—continuing until today just over 3,000 years later—there have only been approximately eighty generations since the giving of the Torah![150]

Logic would dictate that the tradition would have been lost long ago, as Jews were persecuted and exiled throughout the world, dispersed to Africa and Europe, to the Far East and beyond. What keeps a people's identity intact—language, land, and culture—were all lost in exile. There was only one thing that remained a constant for the Jewish people: the Torah and its

---

[150] 80 generations multiplied by 40 (estimated years that parents have been handing down this oral tradition to their children) is 3,200 years, approximately the amount of time since the giving of the Torah (1312 BCE).

commandments. If even one letter of a Torah scroll is missing or damaged, Jewish law deems the entire scroll as null and void. You will find the exact same words in a Torah scroll housed today in a synagogue in California, as one uncovered in an archaeological dig of ancient Israel.

Judaism is not based on blind faith. Even after the miracles of the ten plagues and the splitting of the sea, as well as the numerous miracles that took place in the desert, the Jewish people still did not truly believe in God or his prophet Moses until God revealed His presence and spoke *directly* to them. God revealed His existence to an entire nation, because He didn't expect humans to dedicate themselves in the darkest of times through a faith without knowledge.[151]

Shavuot is a time when we can reinforce our connection to the Torah and that original experience on a little mountain where God called out for a relationship with mankind; when heaven and earth re-connected and the world was changed forever.[152]

Rosh Hodesh—The Light Side of the Moon

The first recorded *mitzvah* given to the Jewish people is to sanctify the occasion each month of seeing a new moon.[153] The sages liken the Jewish mission to the role of a moon. The light we see from the moon is simply

---

[151] We can now address a question posed by many scholars. When transmitting the first and most foundational of the Ten Commandments, the *belief in God*, God says: "I am the Lord your God who took you out of the land of Egypt" (Exodus 20:2). Surely a more powerful reason to believe would have been based on God's forming of the entire universe? Freeing a people from slavery is great but clearly not difficult for God. But God felt that demanding a belief based only on observing the universe was too tall an order. He deemed it necessary to reveal His presence directly before asking for loyalty to His requests. This would give the extra strength for future generations to withstand the excruciating tests and struggles.

[152] When God spoke at Mount Sinai, there was no echo. Godliness permeated the physical matter of the world. From then on, a Mitzvah—an action based on the Torah—would take on a Godly energy (Likutei Sichot, vol. 15, p. 77. Shemot Rabbah 28:6).

[153] And the Lord spoke to Moses and Aaron in the land of Egypt, saying: "This month shall mark for you the beginning of the months; it shall be for you the first of the months of the year" (Exodus 12:1-2).

a *reflection* of the light from the sun. While tiny in comparison to the sun, the moon provides light during the darkest of nights. Each of us, too can reflect God's light into the darkness of the world. Once we illuminate our own lives with Torah values, we can then shine its goodness around us, fulfilling the role of being a "Light unto the Nations."[154]

Just as the moon waxes and wanes, shining brightly and then hiding in darkness, so does the Jewish nation. There has been a constant transition from success to disappointment, oppression to freedom, and destruction to renewal. Every period of darkness is followed by an illumination.

The moon waxes for the first fifteen days of the month, the Jewish people rose in spiritual stature and greatness during their first fifteen generations, from Abraham to King Solomon. Like the full moon, they had reached their *fullness*, shining God's light into the world through the Holy Temple in Jerusalem built by Solomon. Visitors from around the world who arrived in Jerusalem were met with spiritual inspiration and guidance. This was also Israel's most peaceful time in history, when surrounding nations, instead of attacking, visited King Solomon and witnessed the daily miracles in the Temple. The fifteen generations following the reign of Solomon, however, marked a descent full of strife and national divide, like the darkness of the moon during the second half of the month. We may consider ourselves to be tiny and limited beings, but like the small moon, our actions can enable the strongest light to shine into the darkness of our world.

Tu B'av—Love and Reunion

The fifteenth day of the Hebrew month of Av is the holiday of Tu B'av. While this day usually flies under the radar, the Talmud gives it quite a bit of attention: "There were no greater festivals for Israel than the fifteenth of Av and Yom Kippur. On these days, the daughters of Jerusalem would

---

[154] Isaiah 42:6.

go out... and dance in the vineyards."[155] These two days were times of rejoicing when love was in the air, with dancing and many matches made. Why are these two holidays so perfectly suited for love and celebration?

It's especially surprising that people rejoiced in this manner on Yom Kippur, a day known as the holiest and most solemn day of the year! Today, Yom Kippur is marked by fasting, introspection, and long hours of prayer in synagogue.

Once we delve into the events that led to the original Yom Kippur, we begin to understand. After the sin of the golden calf and subsequent days of repentance and remorse, God gave Moses the second tablets to bring back to the people on the tenth day of Tishrei-Yom Kippur. Thus, the theme of this day is forgiveness and closeness, when God and the Jewish nation were reunited in love. This day showed mankind the power of forgiveness, how our relationship with the Divine and with others can not only withstand mistakes, but can become stronger when we feel real remorse and have a strong desire to renew our love. This is why this was a day of such celebration and matchmaking.

Many special events occurred on the fifteenth day of Av, but what is uniquely special about that date and how does it connect to matchmaking? Unlike other holidays, Tu B'av is connected to a darkness that preceded it. The first and second Temples in Jerusalem were destroyed on the same day 490 years apart—the ninth day of *Av*—forever associating this month with a theme of tragedy and spiritual descent. This means that the reunion that occurred on Tu B'av, only six days after the destruction of the Holy Temple, has a unique power. The Sages explain: "The purpose of descent is for the sake of the greater ascent that follows."[156] The further backward a quarterback or pitcher winds their arm, the farther forward the ball flies. The lower you land on a trampoline, the higher you will reach. A muscle torn and then repaired often becomes even stronger after rehabilitation.

---

[155] Taanit 26b.

[156] Likkutei Torah, Vayikra, p. 73a, 77c.

Besides for toxic cases, a renewed relationship after genuine change has the potential to become stronger than ever before.

This is why matches were made on Tu B'av and Yom Kippur. Marriage, as well, isn't a union between two people, but a *reunion*. Originally, a soul is divided into two halves: one half descends from Heaven into one body, the other half into another body.[157] Marriage is the reunion of these two estranged halves.[158] When the two finally find one another, two halves of a soul reunite and become whole. This is why marriage is cause for such grand celebration.[159]

This is what is celebrated on Tu B'av. After the mourning of the Temple's destruction, we rebound and see the deeper reason behind the destruction—the most momentous reconciliation imaginable. While we try our best to avoid falling, it's important to remember that, however low we descend into darkness, an even greater light and ascent awaits us once we decide to change direction. A cold feeling of distance from the Divine that stems from our past mistakes can lead to a warmer, stronger, more loving relationship than ever before.

---

[157] "Forty days prior to the formation of a child, a heavenly voice calls out, saying: 'The daughter of so and so is destined for so and so'" (Sotah 2b).

[158] Originally, this was even expressed physically, as Adam and Eve were joined together back-to-back when created. God then separated Eve from Adam, followed by a reunion. "No female or male soul is complete without the other" (Zohar 1:55b, 3:24a).
Judaism advocates a monthly separation between husband and wife for a short time, known as *Taharat Mishpacha*—Family Purity. This time without physical intimacy during the menstrual cycle, followed by immersion in water known as a *mikvah*, makes room for a renewed passion when reuniting after time apart.

[159] The topic of soul mates is a complex one, explored at length in mystical texts. For example, when two halves of a soul descend into two people, if one of the two has not developed morally and spiritually to the level of the other, it is possible that he or she will not merit to meet the right mate at that time, and the other will meet someone else at his or her current level. Divorce may stem from an unequal level of refinement of character, and that person may end up meeting their true soul mate who has developed their character to an equal level as their partner. Those who haven't yet found mates are encouraged to grow and better their deeds and character, for perhaps they are not yet on the level of their prospective mate who is waiting to meet them.

Afterword
Face to Face

In the summer of 2010, I found myself standing at the Western Wall in the old city of Jerusalem among thousands of people, with CNN cameras in my face. Maybe I should back up a moment. This wasn't any ordinary evening; it was the ninth day of Av, the date commemorating the destruction of both the First Temple (833-423 BCE) and the Second Temple (349-70 BCE) in the old city of Jerusalem. Sadly, many tragedies in history have occurred on this date, such as the expulsion of Jews from Spain in 1492. This day is known as the saddest day of the Jewish year, which is why thousands of people were praying at the Wall on that night.

During the interview, I tried to find the words to explain the significance of the day. How does the ancient destruction of the Temple in Jerusalem affect my life in the twenty-first century? In true Jewish fashion, I began with a question: "If one believes that God is everywhere, as the Zohar states, 'There is no place devoid of Him,'[160] then why do Jewish people pray every day toward Jerusalem? Surely any direction would suffice?"

I asked one more question: "When speaking with a friend, why do we specifically look at the face? If there's a soul and inner life force that encompasses the entire body, it makes as much sense to speak to the feet!"

---

[160] Tikkunei Zohar, Tikkun 57.

The reason is that a person's soul is revealed most in the face. As the saying goes: "The eyes are the windows to the soul."[161] This is the same reason why people pray in one location or toward another, and why Jewish prayer is aimed toward Jerusalem specifically. In Jewish tradition, this is where the divine presence is most revealed and felt most palpably; Jerusalem is the *face of the universe*.

Never was this revelation more clear than during the Temple's existence. There, the spiritual fused with the physical in a seamless manner. All were able to witness God's influence through daily miracles.[162] As our forefather Jacob exclaimed when he first arrived there: "God is truly in this place... How awesome this place is! This is none other than the house of God. This is the gate of heaven."[163] As the Midrash adds: "Jerusalem is the light of the world... and who is the light of Jerusalem? The Holy One, blessed be He."[164]

But do we really miss that era where Godliness was so apparent? Today, the average person in the Western world lives a better life materially than a French king did three hundred years ago. Why would I want an old temple? But this perspective comes from an *exile* mentality, where a divine reality is concealed from our eyes. The Sages describe the exile in which we find ourselves as a "doubled darkness." Why *doubled*? When you're in a dark place, at least you know that you're in darkness. But in the spiritual darkness of today's world, we don't even recognize we're in darkness in the first place! The evil we see in today's world only exists because God hides his presence. In the advanced society of the twenty-first century, we don't feel we're missing out on anything. But many of us lack clarity of

---

[161] Scientists at Orebro University in Sweden compared the eyes of 428 subjects with their personality traits to see if the structures in their irises reflected their characteristics. They found that the patterns in the iris can give an indication of whether we are warm and trusting or neurotic and impulsive!

[162] See Yoma 21a, as one example.

[163] Genesis 28:16-17.

[164] Bereshit Rabbah 59:8.

purpose. Even those who live elevated lives, experiencing spiritual pleasure and moments of transcendence, only taste a tiny morsel of a true reality.

I finished the interview as the sounds of crying prayers from the elderly men and women at the Wall echoed through the night. I could feel in that moment how strongly the world needs God to come out of hiding and bring love, harmony, justice, and inspiration to all. The only way for us to really change this world is through our actions. I pray that each of us find our unique individual purpose in bringing our light to better the world. Only you are capable of making your unique impact and contribution to humanity. If that seems insignificant, who are we to decide which actions are deemed most precious in the eyes of God? Your contribution could make all the difference. As Maimonides teaches: One should see the world and oneself as an equal scale of good and evil. One good deed can tip the scales and bring the redemption![165]

---

[165] Maimonides, Laws of Repentance 3:4.

Acknowledgements

This book is only an interpretation of the lessons I've been privileged to learn over the years. My journey began with the teachings of Rabbi Akiva Tatz and his book *Worldmask*, which greatly influenced my writings. I feel an immense gratitude toward all of my brilliant teachers in yeshiva, led by Rabbi Shmuel Braun and the incredible staff at the Mayanot Institute of Jewish Studies in Jerusalem, who I continually debated with and learned so much from.

A great thanks is owed to my talented and very patient content editor, Zev Gotkin, as well as the insightful Brian Marks. Thank you to my adept grammar editor, Madalyn Stone, and multi-skilled formatter, Jay Polmar.

Thank you to all the friends and family who have supported my journey and given guidance and encouragement along the way, you know who you are.

Much gratitude is owed to my guide, the visionary Lubavitcher Rebbe.

My ultimate thanks and unending love is given to my Creator, who amazes me every day. Thank you for everything.

About the Author

Rabbi Daniel Bortz grew up in San Diego, California. At 19, he left for six years to cities around the world to study Biblical, Talmudic and Jewish mystical teachings in depth. Upon returning to California, he created *JTEEN of San Diego*, an organization that educates and empowers teenagers. Rabbi Bortz is a competitive Brazilian Jiu Jitsu practitioner, and each year serves the needs of thousands of visitors to the Coachella Music festival.

Known to some as the *Millennial Rabbi*, Bortz looks to fuse ancient Jewish wisdom and spirituality with 21st century pop culture, speaking to audiences around the world.

For any thoughts, questions, to book a speaking engagement or watch video illustrations of ideas in this book, please visit: rabbibortz.com
To connect on social media: @rabbibortz

Made in the USA
San Bernardino, CA
28 July 2017